D1230181

Christianity and Modern Crises

Christianity *and* Modern Crises

by

HARRY RIMMER, D.D., LL.D.

SECOND EDITION

WM. B. EERDMANS PUBLISHING COMPANY

Grand Rapids   **1945**   Michigan

CHRISTIANITY AND MODERN CRISES
By HARRY RIMMER, D.D., LL.D.

Copyright, 1944, by
The Research Science Bureau, Inc.

3834

CONTENTS

•

Christianity and Modern Crises

CHAPTER I

THE CHURCH AND ORGANIZED LABOR

IN a sense, the title of this book may be a trifle misleading. The question of the survival of the Church of Christ does not depend upon the attitude and conduct of outside forces and agencies, as history has demonstrated again and again. Despotic governments, vast organized social systems, antagonistic religions, and armed force have all been used to stamp out the Christian belief and revelation, and all have failed most dismally. In the light of our past preservation and in view of the history of revivals, I am sure that Christianity will emerge from its present trials and dangers with its power undimmed and its message unchanged—but only if the leadership of Christendom and the heads of the organized churches awaken to the great crises that face us today. When I speak in these pages of "the Church" and "Christianity" I do not mean the invisible Body of Christ, which is the true and Continuing Church of the New Testament, but rather I refer to the organization of our working forces into the visible and operating corporations which are the traditionally representative bodies of Protestantism. These grim and somber days contain issues which are pregnant with peril for the organized Church. *Basic Christianity is in no danger!*

This is true for many reasons. First, Christianity had an origin which antedates history. Before Adam was created, Christianity was an established principle, program, power, and force in the mind of God, who only awaited the proper moment in history to release and reveal the message and method of redemption rooted in His eternal purposes. This is quite apparent from such passages as we find in the sermon of Peter, as recorded in Acts 2:23."

"Him, being delivered by the determinate counsel and fore-knowledge of God, ye have taken, and by wicked hands have crucified and slain."

Thus the Word of God speaks of the origin of the Gospel message; it was foreknown and planned by God before the dawn of earth's earliest ages. This is the consistent testimony of all the writers of the Bible, and we have no other source of knowledge concerning God, His plans for men, the Gospel and its content. Hence we are limited in our proper concep-tions of Christianity by the contests of the Revelation, and any idea of the Gospel which differs from the written Word is a false idea and cannot be accepted by any true Christian. And this fact of the origin of our Faith antedating history is one of the common propositions of the Bible.

Jesus so taught when He said that in His teachings He would utter things "which have been kept secret from the foundations of the world." In His Olivet discourse, Jesus prophesied that in His return and at the judgment of that hour, He would say to the deserving, "Come, ye blessed of my Father, inherit the kingdom prepared for you from the foundation of the world."

The Apostle Paul had this fact in mind when he wrote to the Church at Ephesus:

"According as He hath chosen us in Him before the foundation of the world."

And Peter also agrees with this fact, for he writes about our redemption through the blood of Christ, our Lamb,

"Who verily was foreordained before the foundation of the world, but was manifest in these last times for you."

Twice in the book of The Revelation, John, the favored friend of Jesus, made mention of the pre-historic origin of our

Faith, when he told of "The book of the Lamb slain from the foundation of the world."

Since we were not born in history, we shall not perish while history persists—our destiny is hid with Christ in God!

Then note that this pre-determined Faith was announced through the Prophets. And since prophecy is the voice of God, whose words are eternal and changeless, the utterances of men who prophesied the rule and extent of the Church partake of finality. This promised salvation was announced in Jesus Christ, purchased on Calvary, established by our Lord's resurrection, attested by His ascension, is now administered from Heaven, and will be consummated in the Kingdom of God! How then can such a system fail?

Since such a system is not dependent upon either human agencies or corporation, Christianity is as eternal as its Source and Administrator. Being administered by the Holy Spirit, Christianity is safe in spite of the strength of the foes and the weakness of its friends, and we have no questions or fears about the future of the Christian Faith.

The organized Church of the twentieth century is quite different! Being human in origin, it is fallible in nature, and may well lose its grip upon civilization, even as it has forfeited its once complete leadership in the United States of America. The last twenty-five years have seen the decay of the power and influence of the Protestant Churches to such an extent that they are no longer the chief factors in our national life, as they were in the days of our parents! The reasons for this decline are many, chief of which are apostasy and prosperity. The great denominations have been infiltrated with agnosticism and doubt to such an extent that many of them no longer deserve the name "Christian." The leaders of strong organizations have repudiated the Gospel which was the sole source of the power of the Church. Having millions at their disposal, these same leaders found themselves "rich and in need of nothing," so that they became arrogant and callous to the cry of orthodoxy, sweeping us all into an orgy of social service and educational endeavor that had no place in the plans for a redemptive Gospel. In so doing the Church lost touch with the common people, and empty pews resulted. We squandered fortunes upon imposing buildings, ornate with artistic beauty, but cold and harsh to the poor and needy. I have seen churches whose cost of construction would have equaled the entire missionary budget of their denomination for ten years, and a hundred and fifty worshipers were all who gathered to hear the sermon and worship on the Lord's Day! The cars they rode in and the clothes and ornaments worn by the women would have evangelized a great city, and the poor and humble would no more have entered those portals than a fish would have left the water!

This condition constitutes an anomaly: it is a negation of Christianity and an indictment of the organized denominations. We have apparently forgotten the manner and nature of our origin. The first "church members" were slaves, laborers, fishermen, and mechanics. The poor and humble made up our ranks to the extent that Paul could truthfully write to an early church:

"But witness your own calling brethren, how that not many wise men after the flesh, not many mighty, not many noble . . . ."

and that was the general rule of the primitive and apostolic church. Through all the ages the mass of our membership has been drawn from the ranks of the common people, and that is one of the secrets of our great success!

There is something wrong with a church that loses touch with the laboring masses. I worked for my daily bread at hard labor; didn't you? I have plowed, planted, and reaped. I have swung an axe in the woods and operated every machine in the mill. For years I carried a card of membership in a labor union; in fact I have belonged to two of them. I glory in the fact that I could start out today and practice either one of two trades, and earn my livelihood at the bench or by my hands. When I go to shop meetings I can preach to the boys in their own language: I can show a scar that came to me in an accident in the mill, and bear in my body the proof of years of toil. Why shouldn't a preacher be proud of the fact that he also labored? Our Founder grew up in a carpenter shop, and He often wiped the bitter sweat from His brow as He toiled at His tasks. There is something radically wrong with any organized church whose membership is not composed largely of men and women who *work!*

This was once the common and general rule, but in our own generation Labor Unions have *dis*-placed and *re*-placed the Church in the lives and thinking of the working masses. The affectionate loyalty that mechanics once manifested toward their place of worship has largely shifted to their trade unions, and the working man is conspicuous in the modern churches by his absence! I dare assert that not more than five per cent of the entire membership of any labor union habitually attends church!

What has brought this regrettable condition to pass? Has the saving Gospel of Jesus Christ lost its appeal to common folks? No, it has not, and when and where the redeeming Grace of Christ is preached clearly and positively it allures and wins lost men of every class. I recently held some special services in a stately church in a northern city, and when the services had closed one night a very imposing lady came up to me and said in agitated tones, "Dr. Rimmer, did you see those five men in the back of our church *dressed in overalls?*" "No," I replied, "I didn't happen to notice them. But what is wrong with that? Didn't Jesus die for folks in overalls as well as for those who wear broadcloth and ermine?"

In tones of sincere emotion the lady answered: "There is *nothing* wrong with that! Of course Christ died for all men: but that's the first time in twelve years I've ever seen workingmen in our grand church! I'm so happy over it I could weep!"

It would be a marvelous thing if more church members felt this same way. The winsome call of the Saviour of the world is given without respect of persons, apart from class, and with no restrictions regarding wealth, culture, or social standing. There is something vitally wrong with any religious organization that has lost its grip on the men and women who build and produce: they are the people who make the nation, and it cannot be denied that the overwhelming majority of the membership of the greater trade unions are totally uninterested in work, worship, and service of the Protestant churches.

There are three main reasons for this terrible present indifference, as a careful survey of the recent past will clearly show. The first cause lies in education. The schooling of the masses is derived from the great system of public schools, of which America is justly proud. In an earlier day teachers were men and women who uniformly professed and practiced the Christian faith, held up a high example of moral conduct, and lived out their confession. In such times our instructors molded our minds into thought patterns that produced character, formed real citizens, and naturally led to reverence. But the opposite condition exists today, and American educators are undermining our national faith.

An animalistic philosophy of origin has displaced the fact of creation in the earlier grades, the Bible is either totally ignored in a majority of our public schools or else it is derided, scoffed at, and ridiculed. It is quite beyond reason to expect that a child will attend school seven hours a day for five days in the week and hear the Bible disputed, then go to church on *one* day for *one* hour and maintain a reverence for the Holy Word. Of course, there are exceptions to this general condition, especially in our southern states. I have often lectured and preached in school assemblies where the Bible was read and prayer offered by the faculty members, but such is not the universal rule in the nation as it was in our own youth. Educators have been widely responsible for the collapse in faith, morals, and conduct in this generation. You can't teach men and women that they are animals and expect them to act like the sons of God! Hence our children grow up in homes founded by parents who are the victims of a false philosophy of education, and the present lack of restraint is the inevitable end of this sad condition.

The second reason for the indifference of the working masses to the claims of the church is the fact that communism seized control and leadership of the unions in the recent period of astonishing expansion under governmental favor and pampering. Thus the chief enemies of Christianity were in a strategic position to spread atheism in the ranks of labor, and they made good use of their opportunities. They must be commended for their forethought and perspicacity.

When the sudden boom came in trade unions, they were the only group which was alert to the situation and prepared to take advantage of the trend. Indeed, they planned for it long in advance, and had a great part in bringing this great union movement to fruition. They had their leaders trained and established in places of leadership and influence, and while Communists are a very minor proportion of the entire membership in any union, they hold the reigns in many unions.

The philosophy of Communism exalts the present world and derides the idea of a life to come. The common cry of the communist is, "I don't want pie in the sky bye and bye: I want chicken on the table right now;" Communism believes and teaches that religion is an opiate for the conscience of the race, something that Capitalism invented to keep the people who work contented in the chains of industrial slavery. It forgets that the Christian religion was founded by a Carpenter, promulgated by commercial fishermen, laborers and slaves, and that the history of Christianity is just the record of the redemption and elevation of the masses of humanity. But by subtle propaganda communistic leaders have mislead the labor movement into a position of opposition to the Church and all for which it stands.

The final reason for our present sad state of estrangement is the most important, being the fact that the organized church lost its zeal and enthusiasm for evangelism. It is exiomatic that a cold church cannot kindle a flame in the hearts of its prospects! The organized church has been asleep, and it is her own fault that she has allowed the gross things of the flesh to make inroads in the spheres where spiritual interests should predominate. Communism in all of its phases would beat a hasty retreat before the advance of an aggressive church which believed and preached salvation through the shed blood of the Lamb of God. But the leaders of the great denominations have laid aside this old-fashioned message; they have repudiated the God-given and time-tested method of evangelism, and as a natural and inevitable consequence we have lost our grip upon the affections of the common people.

I do not believe it is necessary to argue that fact: the estrangement between labor and the church is so apparent it must be conceded. There are local exceptions of course, but the general picture is dark indeed. In a recent campaign in the City of Detroit we had crowds in attendance which number- ed from two to three thousand a night ,but they were largely the so-called "white collar" classes. The teeming throngs of the A. F. of L. and the C. I. O. were represented by a dozen, or at most a score.

Can the church regain this lost influence with organized labor?

She must — or perish!

The organized church cannot long exist apart from the laboring classes. Our ranks are recruited in each generation from those who toil, and our destiny is closely allied to the progress and aid of the common folks. These are the "goodly" folks, the stable and consistent folks, the very people God loved with a deep affection, and the ones for whom Christ died! So for the sake of our own future we must make a determined effort to win back our forfeited prestige with labor, or we are doomed as an organization.

The re-habilitation of the fellowship between the Church and labor is equally important for the future of trade unions. For if the Church cannot prosper without the aid of labor, neither can the unions exist without the Church! There are two sides to this problem, and labor leaders would do well to consider their aspect of the issue with the same honesty that we display when we examine our position. Apart from a Christian state labor unions are doomed, and if the Church goes down all of the structures of democracy will crash with her. Our interest and concern over the situation are not purely selfish. We recognize the great contribution which organized labor can make to the social welfare of our people, and we desire that progress which can be so achieved, but we also know that in non-Christian countries labor unions are not tolerated. We shall advance proof of that later in this book; here we merely state the inescapable fact that our destinies are entwined so closely that the Church and labor have equal need of each other.

We can find a renewal of that mutual aid and comfort which marked our earlier history and association if we follow the proper technique. Where there is a dislocation, the correct remedy is re-location. Since there are three things wrong in the immediate picture, the simplest way to recovery is to correct those three errors. Together the organized Church and organized labor constitute a majority in America. And, since we are a democracy, the majority is presumed to be in control. Let us unite to demand that educators cease their vicious campaign of instruction that undermines faith, and if necessary compel them to stick to their proper subjects of classroom teaching. There is a difference between "academic freedom" in which we all believe, and license to propagate personal philosophies and false theories that wreck ideals and lives. We should purge education of unworthy educators and get back into the channels of thought which produced the characteristics of sterling quality which made our fathers and mothers men and women of stability.

The second step is to thrust communists and racketeers out of the leadership of such trade unions as may be dominated by them, and get leaders of truly American ideals into the seats of power. The men who steer the bark of labor are the ones who guide its progress and determine its goals. Why have crafty advocates of European systems at the head of American institutions? Let us help each other by re-annunciating the simple principles of faith and brotherhood, once borrowed from the Church and now ignored by those who plagerized Christian premises to deceive American labor. Like wolves garbed in sheep's pelts, Communists made their great gain in our ranks by disguising their real nature and purpose. Now intrenched and emboldened Communism advances its aims of atheism and denounces the Church and the very liberty our system makes possible.

Above all, let us call the Church back to the old paths, and rekindle in her the evangelistic passion which once marked her as a divine institution. If a real revival *could* sweep the religious bodies of America which call themselves by the name of Christ, but preach any Gospel *except* His, the fires kindled in our local congregations would soon set our communities on fire to such a extent that we would quickly awaken the nation.

Honest confession is like good diagnosis. You can't treat a sickness properly until you know what the ailment is, and the same rule applies to recovery and revival. It is with considerable shame and even more sadness that we confess that the organized Church has failed organized labor. We believe we can do better, if our own leaders will quit "searching for new truth" and begin to proclaim the *old* Truth which has always proved its power to set men free.

Now how about the labor movement? How do trade unions stand in the public esteem today? What future does organized labor have in our democracy? Is there nothing wrong with its present conduct, and has it no faults to correct?

Do the labor unions dare to be as honest in confession as we have been?

It is apparent to the most casual observer that all is not serene or perfect in the ranks of labor. There are rumblings of a popular revolt against the arbitrary despotism of labor, and an aroused Republic is slowly moving to a wrathful explosion. This is one reason why we say labor needs the aid of the Church, unless the trade unions clean their own house the termites they have so complacently harbored will destroy their entire edifice!

If the leaders of labor had the best interests of the working man at heart, they could profit greatly by making an honest investigation to procure facts wherewith to answer our final pertinent query, which is, "How does organized labor stand today in the esteem of the general public?" This is a most important issue, since in our form of government the aroused populace can crush any movement of which it disapproves, can handicap with rigid laws and stern regulations any organization or group, or can promote with its approval and favor such issues as the populace feels are justified of their support and commendation. And when we check the cross-currents of American opinion today, trade unions are treated as objects of suspicion and are subject to the keenest scrutiny from eyes that are far from friendly.

The chief reason for this general attitude of condemnation is the fact that certain sad and shabby pages mar the war record of organized labor. We are not forgetting the miracle of industrial production which helped to save our manner of life for the present, and we have all honor to pay to those citizens, either in management or production, who have contributed their best to the war effort. *More* could not be expected—*less* is treason! The story of labor's magnificent achievement is marred and blotted by a dismal succession of strikes in war plants and vital industries, all of which have set back the hour of victory by the exact amount of time lost from production. This loss must be paid for in the somber coin of the bloody wounds and physical suffering of fighting men. Most of these strikes have been called for selfish reasons, inspired by the agreed for gain, prestige, or power of a limited number within labor's ranks. This fact can be illustrated by one specimen case out of many.

In the month of May, 1944, all of the allied peoples were waiting in dread for the zero hour of the impending "D" day. Our sons and brothers were poised to hurl their living bodies against the grim and skilfully prepared defences of the European fortresses, and we were sure that a horrible price must be paid for success in that venture. Our prayers and hopes rode with the gallant lads of the air forces who daily and nightly blasted the enemy emplacements, factories, communications and positions, for we well knew that their success meant the saving of countless lives. Three thousand, five hundred foremen took this time to go out on strike, condemning sixty thousand workers in airplane production to forced idleness! These foremen were quite contented with their wages, hours, working conditions, and benefits; they just wanted recognition of their union! And because they were not granted this, they calmly, coldly, selfishly, and unpatriotically shut off the production of the fighters and bombers we so desperately needed. In spite of directives from the War Labor Board and appeals from the President, these men persisted in their work stoppage for twenty days. They surrendered then only because General Arnold, commanding the Air Force of the entire United States, appeared before the executive committee of the striking union and bluntly told them that their treasonable conduct was hindering the invasion plans, and that unless production was resumed thousands of American lives would be lost on European beach heads! Yielding to this pressure, the union voted to allow the resumption of the production of planes for the embattled United States forces.

Get out your pencil and paper and do a little simple arithmetic. Sixty thousand men were idle twenty days. At an average working day of eight hours, that is *four hundred eighty thousand man-hours lost each day!* The time required for the manufacture of a bomber is now thirteen thousand hours, so this strike robbed the air force of five hundred and fifty three planes in the twenty days that the strike lasted. THAT IS OVER TWO HUNDRED MORE THAN WE LOST BY ENEMY ACTION IN ALL THEATRES OF BATTLE IN THAT SAME TWENTY DAYS! In other words, the very men for whom our sons are fighting injured them more in those dark twenty days than the enemy did. Is *any* gain made by any group worth that fearful price? And how can organized labor justify this conduct to the fighting men when they return and demand a reckoning?

Frankly and fearlessly we proclaim an undeniable truth: *in a nation at war the individual has no rights!* "Social gains," "living standards," "free speech," "constitutional guarantees" and all the other safe-guards of normal living are properly suspended when a nation fights for its very existence. What would become of all of our freedoms and if we lost the war?

They would be swept away until such time as we could win them back by force of arms. Consider this forfeiture of rights as it applies to the case of every soldier. A draft act is passed, and the Government seizes the very person of a citizen and puts him into uniform. Immediately he loses his individuality and all of his personal rights. He cannot appeal to the civil courts, he has no habeas corpus proceedings to safeguard his person, he can be imprisoned at the will of his company commander. He can be punished without trial, and his freedom of speech is so absolutely dissipated that he can't even talk back to a sergeant! He cannot bargain either individually or collectively for better conditions of work, wage, or housing; he takes what is given him by governmental decree and likes it—or else!

Further, in drafting him for *your* defense, the authorities may completely destroy his business, and for the time of his employment as a soldier break up his home. Without his own consent he is torn from the arms of his wife and separated from parents or children, and is ordered to live for months or years in an alien land where he is viewed and hated as an enemy. And if he doesn't like any of this and attempts to organize a strike in protest, he is shot!

Now consider the worker on the production line, for whom the soldier is fighting. Why should not the Government have the same powers over him that it exercises over the soldier? Is there some magic difference between overalls and Khaki? Blue denim or olive darb should not make this vast disparity: the country belongs to all of us, and we should all be in her service when she needs our aid. If the government can rightfully draft the fighter, as we concede it may properly do, why cannot it also draft the mechanic? The man who goes out to bleed and die in his country's cause should stand on a footing, that is at least equal to that of the mechanic who builds or produces for the same cause.

I dare labor to face its own record here! Can you picture what would have happened in the Pacific theatre of war if General MacArthur had been forced to reckon with *millions of hours,* of "absenteeism" among his fighting forces? A soldier or sailor who over-stays his scanty leave is harshly punished —the worker who disrupts the production line while he idles or recovers from a drinking bout is pampered, coddled, and put back into action. This is manifestly unfair.

In addition to this, output of vital equipment is limited by labor rules which restrict production in order to serve individual greed. And in so stating, I am not advancing any personal opinion, but merely summarizing the facts as they can be gleaned from any newspaper, for the conversations of indignant citizens of every class, and from the editorial comment of the entire country. If labor leaders do not know of the tidal wave of angry retribution now building up against them, they are either blind or deaf, and perhaps a little of both! The working masses which follow them will also suffer greatly in a day of judgment that is anything but distant, for even though blind followers may blame blind leaders when they all fall into the ditch together, the followers still have the bumps and the bruises!

The situation at the present hour grows progressively worse instead of getting better. There are more strikes instead of fewer, and the more certain classes of workers get the more they want. And to procure their personal desires they do not hesitate to tie up plants, factories, or transportation systems to the great aid and comfort to the enemy. To illustrate this trend, and the dangerous increase in work stoppage, let me present a simple factual report in the following newspaper clipping from Michigan:

"STATE LABOR ROWS SHOWN INCREASING"

"Lansing—(AP)—The state labor mediation board said Thursday its monthly summary disclosed a rise in the number of strikes and unsettled labor disputes in Michigan in December as compared with November and a larger number of persons affected by the strikes.

"The survey showed 56 strikes occurred in December, affecting 30,706 employes, compared with 47 strikes affecting 17,095 employes in November.

"Entering December with a case load of 292 labor disputes the board received notice of 90 new disputes, recorded settlement of 82 disputes and entered the new year with 300 unsettled ones on its books.

"There was 228 unsettled disputes at the start of November, 117 new disputes recorded and 53 cases closed."

Analyze those figures and note their tremendous significance, remembering that they constitute the record of only one state in the Union. This hard-pressed group of public-spirited men who constitute the State Labor Meditation Board (incidentally soldiers, sailors, and marines have no "mediation boards" or "grievance committees" to "mediate" between them and their commanding officers: they do as they are told) when the month of November began, was carrying a load of 292 "labor disputes" to which was added 90 *new disputes* in that month. They settled 82 of the arguments, and at the start of the new year had 300 fights still pending: a clear gain to the enemy of exactly 8 cases that added to the long list of industrial sabotage. Someone in Michigan certainly deserves the Iron Cross or the Order of the Japanese Empire, third class, for this efficient impediment to America's fight for her life. While this total covers *just one state,* it must be remembered that the state in question is Michigan, which probably produces more armament and vital war supplies than any other state in the union.

I stated in a previous paragraph that *greed* was at the basis of most of these disputes. Read this short article from a Detroit paper and see what my premise really is:

"PREPARING FINDINGS ON GM CONTRACT ROW"

"DETROIT—(AP)—A special national war labor board tripartite panel Thursday began preparing its findings on a contract renewal dispute hearing between General Motors corporation and the United Automobile Workers (CIO) for submittal within four weeks to the national WLB.

"Demands for the union's withdrawal of opposition to incentive pay plans were argued by General Motors spokesmen at the closing session of the hearings.

"The spokesmen contended that incentive pay had increased production from 37 to 50 per cent at the Aero Products division at Dayton, Ohio.

"Walter P. Reuther, union vice president and director of the GM council, asserted the union's opposition was based on fear of employes they would work themselves out of jobs. He said that 1,200 employes of GM's Oldsmobile division in Lansing were laid off Tuesday because of lack of work and that employes of other GM plants where incentive pay systems are operative have requested the WLB to place them back on an hourly rate wage schedule because they do not receive earnings as high as formerly under hourly rates."

This action by the CIO is one of the most dis-heartening and questionable acts so far published. Think this issue through item by item and you have a glaring example of greed and selfish interests ignoring the national welfare. The General Motors Corporation discovered a simple method of overcoming slow-downs in production: they established a system of bonus pay for excess production in vital war materials. In some plants this resulted in an increase of from thirty-seven percent and in another the acceleration was sixty-one percent! That means that every soldier could have from thirty-seven to sixty-one extra rounds of ammunition for every one hundred he had been getting, that the Air Corps could have a hundred and fifty planes in the same period of time they formerly used to receive one hundred. For every hundred bombs dropped on the enemy they could now have a hundred and fifty, and the famine of supplies could soon be overcome at that rate.

This grand progress was halted by the union leaders on the grounds that the men employed "might" work themselves out of a job! The lads at Cassino and Anzio Beachhead are not worried about doing so much they will have no more to do! Why should the laborers who supply them with the sinews of war act and think any differently? Is this *their* war, or ours? The union bases its argument on the fact that in one plant 1,200 men were laid off when they got too far ahead of schedule. Well, that ought to be easy to remedy! If those idle men cannot be employed in other lines of war work, send them to Italy to replace 1,200 weary and worn fighting men who would be glad for a short lay-off! These muddy, exhausted, wounded and desperate men who *cannot* quit would gladly trade places, I am sure.

The position of the union is that there is just so much material required in the years of the war: if they make it all now there will soon be no need for their labor. But our harrassed fighters don't want this material *next* year *they want it now!* And without it they may die. "Well, let them," says a certain variety of labor leader, "We have to protect our jobs and our incomes!"

Even worse than personal greed as a motive in war-time strikes is the incentive of prestige. When working conditions are as near to ideal as it is possible to make them, and when hours and pay are completely satisfactory, one would think strikes in war industries would never occur. But they do! The prestige and privilege of collecting dues from thousands of workers naturally means much to labor leaders; apparently far more than the security of their beleaguered nation! Consider this news item:

"THREATS, REPROACHES, GREET WAR STRIKERS" BARD APPEALS TO LOYALTY; WLB URGES PENALTIES

"DETROIT, Feb. 5 — (AP) — Reproaches from spokesmen for the armed forces and Government agencies today confronted about 25,000 war plant strikers in Michigan and Ohio along with a War Labor Board threat of full sanctions and penalties. "The strike, begun yesterday, was that of members of the Independent Mechanics Educational Society of America who walked out in Cleveland, Detroit and elsewhere protesting the National Labor Relations Board's *handling of a jurisdictional issue.*" A demand that the men return to work as a condition of loyalty to their country was voiced by Ralph A. Bard, acting Secretary of the Navy. Referring to necessary equipment for invasion forces, Bard said the strike was greatly increasing the hazards of our war effort.

"The acting secretary telegraphed his demand to Matthew Smith, national secretary of the unions, at the time the War Labor Board was threatening sanctions and ordering a hearing in Washington on Monday.

"Smith, in defiance, tacitly invited the board to apply sanctions and asserted the strike would continue."

The one question involved in this case is that of jurisdiction. The burning issue is, "The members of which union shall be employed in what capacity?" This carries with it, of course, the equally important question of which financial coffer shall reap the usual per centum of tribute in the form of dues. So *twenty-five thousand men* lay down their tools in vital defense plants, and refuse to work when their leader gives the signal. The Federal commission points out the fact that this action constitutes disloyalty to the United States, and the Federal authority is *defied* by the union's secretary! Twenty-five thousand men are almost a division and a half in army formations: what sort of a cry would go up in America if that many soldiers refused to fight because they felt they should be doing the job some other outfit was assigned to accomplish? It is a grim fact that since Pearl Harbor there have been jurisdictional strikes which number *hundreds!*

The only strike cause more reprehensible than this is the so-called "sympathy strike." Men who are perfectly contented with their own contracts and conditions, and who have entered into a solemn "no-strike pledge" with the American people, lay down their tools and quit work because *someone else* strikes in some other city! The following item is typical of this situation:

"HINTS 20,000 TO WALK OUT"

"DETROIT, January 17, 1944—(AP)—Robert H. Keys, president of the Foreman's Association of America (independent), asserted Monday that 20,000 organized foremen in Detroit's area war plants were prepared to walk out in sympathy with striking foremen from four divisions of Chrysler corporation, seeking union recognition.

"Keys made his statement at a strikers' meeting after announcing that Chrysler corporation had refused to meet with him. The corporation, he said, referred to the contention it had presented to the war labor board that its foremen are part of management.

"Keys estimated that more than 900 foremen had quit work in two Chrysler-operated Dodge plants and two similarly operated De Soto factories.

("The plants are engaged in production of assemblies for heavy bombers, tanks, guns, tank destroyers and trucks.)

"A company spokesman reiterated the management refusal to recognize the foreman's association as bargaining agency for men it regarded as part of management personnel and said no grievance had been presented."

Here is a factory engaged in making the most essential equipment that soldiers need and cry for, such things as assemblies for heavy artillery, bombers, tanks and tank destroyers. For want of just such equipment France fell, and the lack of French heavy armament was caused by the willful and bitter self-interest of the organized labor groups in France. Foremen are the most important group in any factory; they keep the assembly lines rolling on schedule and direct the work of hundreds of men. Yet twenty thousand "organized" foremen in the Detroit area of the war plants think so little of their country's peril that they will walk out and leave soldiers stranded without the tools of combat simply to aid some other group which is fighting for its own selfish interests!

The action of the group that initiated this shameful condition is reported as follows:

"ELEVEN CHRYSLER PLANTS AFFECTED BY WALKOUT"

"DETROIT—(AP)—Approximately 1,100 members of the Foreman's Association of America (independent) remained away from their jobs at 11 Chrysler corporation plants Thursday pending union-demanded clarification of the war labor board's stand.

"A telegram from the WLB in Washington Wednesday to Robert H. Keys, president of the FAA, said the war and navy departments believed the strike was "effecting an appreciable slowdown of production.

"This strike must be ended immediately," the telegram said. "You are requested to convey to each employe engaged in this work stoppage the instructions of the war labor board that he return to his job immediately."

("Keys, in a telegram of reply, asked clarification, pointing out that we need to know whether it is a directive and order.)

Our position, Keys said later, is that if it is an order and directive then the WLB has assumed jurisdiction. If it is a simple request then the WLB has not assumed jurisdiction and without jurisdiction there is no authority."

All that these men want is *personal recognition* and the right to bargain for future issues which may or may not arise at some indefinite time, and for this they are perfectly willing to cripple the war effort and to defy the Government of the United States! No wonder millions of men in uniform are bitterly enquiring of each other if such a system is *worth* defending!

We have already referred to the strike begun on February fifth, involving a jurisdictional quarrel, in which the union implicated claimed the right to be recognized as sole bargaining agency in the field. In plain language this means they alone could collect dues and level tribute upon the multiplied thousands of men who work in that particular craft. On the seventh of February the agency of the Federal Government, which was empowered to handle such issues, subpoenaed the two principal officers of the union and prepared to hold a hearing. Instead of obeying the subpoenas, the union sent its attorney to represent it, and the attorney informed the War Labor Board that they had no power to terminate *this* strike, only the union's national administrative board could do that! He then said that the Federal authorities would have to "co-operate with" the Union! and threatened a prolonged strike unless the War Labor Board would give in. When he was asked why the President and the Secretary of the Union had failed to appear in answer to the legal summons, this attorney had the insolence to inform the Labor Board that these officers would have to get permission of their own executive council before they could obey the law! You think, perhaps, that this is an exaggeration? Well, read the account for yourself:

TOOL STRIKE'S END PUT UP TO WLB; UNION COUNSEL SUGGESTS CO-OPERATION BY AGENCY; ORDER TO WORK ISSUED

WASHINGTON, Feb. 7—(AP)—Counsel for the Mechanics Educational Society of America intimated at a War Labor Board hearing today that the end of a strike in 44 Michigan and Ohio war plants, involving 25,000 workers, *depends on co-operation from the WLB.*

William L. Brooker, MESA attorney, told the board that only the union's national administrative board can order the strike terminated and added that if the WLB "will co-operate I think this can be terminated in a few hours. If it has to be prolonged it will be prolonged."

He was not asked what form that co-operation would have to take, but union officials have called for a WLB order freezing MESA's status as bargaining representative in the struck plants, which is the central issue of the strike.

Chairman Davis Dissatisfied

The exchange came after William H. Davis, chairman of the WLB, had told Brooker that his appearance at the hearing was not a satisfactory response to subpenas for the two principal officers of the union.

The attorney said Matthew Smith, general secretary, and George White, president, could not attend the hearing without permission of the union's administrative board, now meeting in Cleveland.

Davis replied by reading the law and remarking drily, "I see nothing in the statute about the executive council of the MESA."

Smith and White said in Cleveland that they were ignoring the WLB order to come here.

Later a deputy U. S. marshal interrupted a special meeting of the executive board of the MESA in Cleveland to serve new subpenas on White and Smith.

Called for Tomorrow

Hugh McNamee, chief regional WLB enforcement attorney, said both subpenas directed the unionists to appear before the WLB in Washington tomorrow afternoon.

Davis, after recessing the hearing briefly while the WLB met in executive session, announced that the hearing would be continued until 2:30 P. M. tomorrow. He said the board's legal department has been instructed to do whatever is legally necessary to get compliance. He said the board also had adopted a resolution calling upon the MESA leadership to forthwith call off the strike.

Senator Ferguson (R-Mich.) asked the Department of Justice to investigate the action of Smith and White.

"This is a serious situation, amounting to a strike against the Government," said Ferguson.

He asked for an inquiry into the possibility that Smith's refusal to obey the subpena was in violation of Federal conspiracy statutes and of Federal laws against interfering with the functions of Government boards and courts.

To summarize the situation, compare the condition of February 1943 with the record of the same month in 1944.

February 1943, 40,000 workers idle in labor rows; these strikers piling up the sad total of 120,000 man days! That is the equivalent of about *three hundred and fifty years of labor for one man!*

But in February 1944, there were 115,000 workers on strike, who lost a total of 470,000 man days of production. Think of the ammunition that could be produced for hard-pressed soldiers in almost a half-million days of labor! Ten per cent of the equipment lost through this sad type of treason would have enabled the men who defended the Bataan Peninsula to have held out until help reached them.

Who is to blame for this situation? Some commentators blame the workers, but we must look deeper than that. These strikers are, generally speaking, average Americans. They are the fathers, brothers, mothers, and wives of the very men they are thus betraying. Most of them *want* to work, day and night, if need be, to bring victory to our arms. But they are powerless to exert any initiative—if they do not obey the orders of the labor union executives they are cast out of the organization, and their means of livelihood is thus gone. They have been regimented, hand-cuffed, and delivered bodily into the hands of professional labor leaders whose chattels they have thus become. We cannot lay the initial blame upon the men who strike.

Nor can the chief fault be charged to the union organizers and officials. While it is true that there is a large number of racketeers in certain unions, they are not in the majority. Ex-convicts, gangsters, and crooks have fouled the nest of labor, and labor will some day pay bitterly for allowing this condition to exist, but there are many grand and high-minded men in the labor unions. These distinguished leaders are men of vision who desire the ultimate good of their followers and fellows, and they would lay down their lives for the cause they love and serve. We cannot blame them for the sad record the unions have made in their unpatriotic squabbles and wranglings in the present crisis,—some of them deplore the situation as much as we do.

The fundamental fault lies in our Federal Administration. Official Washington has been far more concerned with politics than it has been with speedy and immediate victory, and the war and its progress have been betrayed by bureaucrats and social reformers for the advancement of personal political ambitions and political philosophies. The Federal Government literally hog-tied labor and delivered it into the hands of racketeers who were shrewd and powerful enough to influence the New Deal toward their own ends and interests. The conservative and constructive union chiefs are all aware of this and are quite outspoken in their condemnation of the inept handling of the situation. There have been too many bungling fingers tangling up the threads of labor's pattern!

John P. Frey, President of the Metal Trades Dept. of the A. F. L. made the direct assertion that there is no central agency to which labor can go with its problems and plans; that no bureau or set of officials can give a definite understanding on labor's difficulties, its rights and its obligations. He states that there are more than *twenty-five different agencies* now regulating terms of employment and working conditions! To quote his words:

"Our labor relationship is the very opposite of that existing in Great Britain, where all labor questions must go through the clearing house of the Minister of Labor."

To show just *how* different our jumbled and confused situation is, make your own list of the alphabetical madhouse Washington has erected to house our labor relations! I have before me as I write, an incomplete list of such agencies, totaling twenty-seven different groups, all of them working independently of each other, and often in antagonism to each other. The Department of Labor *should* be the central and authoritative source of aid to labor, but has less actual authority than any of the others, and is itself divided into five separate sections, the C. S., B. L. S., C. B., W. B., and W. H. D. being the official letters denominating each section

Exceeding them in authority is the N. W. L. B., which presumably settles wage disputes, controls wages, operates through the Labor Department's C. S. in preliminary investigations, but uses its own Regional Boards for final solution of problems. It operates as a fact-finding agency, prosecuting attorney, judge, jury, appellate court, and executioner! Railroad workers are exempt from their rule and authority, and live under the jurisdiction of the more ancient and honorable National Medication Board, which was set up by specific law before the war began.

Independent of all other agencies and commissions, the National Labor Relations Board seeks to effect collective bargaining contracts and arrangements. But the Office of Economic Stabilization can cancel and nullify the work of all of these preceding authorities, exercising veto power over their decisions by virtue of its power to refuse wage increase, if the director of said O. E. S. believes such an increase will upset his personal ideas of price control!

It would be tiresome to list all twenty-seven, especially when we realize that these bureaus are not the primary cause of the confusion and uncertainty: the roots of the matter go into the White House. The present administration is not completely dedicated to the winning of the war, but its chief concern is in perpetuating itself in office. To the White House, politics mean more than immediate victory. This idea is not original with me: millions of my fellow Americans are saying the same thing. Parents all over this land think of their sons and daughters in uniform and resent the fact that the White House applies the standard of sacrifice and service to our fighting forces, but to labor it applies the standard of *votes!* Why this double standard? It is not the soldier's war: it is a war for the defense and protection of civilians!

So to maintain the political co-operation of labor, our President has often undermined his own appointed boards and agencies, giving *favors* to specially strong labor groups in return for their continued friendship. Hence a political machine, guided only by the principle of expediency, has been erected and has functioned where a clearly defined policy should have been. History will bear out this assertion, and the grim betrayal of a nation's interest in the dispensing of political favors will be a sad mark on the record when it is compiled for the next generation. Labor leaders, in the meantime, feel that they have no source of finality, and no central authority in which they can have confidence. If a rival leader has access to the back door of the White House *he* gets what *he* wants (in return for certain favors, of course) and the rest of labor is betrayed.

Thus the administration, in the long issue, becomes the enemy of *both* labor and management. This is ever the case when democracy is betrayed into a bureaucracy. If an employer tries to be fair and generous with business, he is penalized by the government for "violating" the "directives" of some bureau! Certain firms, appreciating the fine loyalty and sacrificial service of their employees—many of them skilled workers who could not be replaced—raised the salaries of such men to share with them the sudden prosperity brought about by increase of business due to the war boom. This was fine and generous, and was the sort of "golden rule" procedure which should solve all labor relations peacefully and justly. But the net result was governmental action against the "criminal" employers who had dealt so generously with their employees! Working through the machinery of the income tax section of the Collector of Internal Revenue, the Regional War Labor Board fined each firm from $2,400 to $20,000 for "violating the law"! I know that this sounds like a page out of "Alice in Wonderland" and, lest you think I concocted the illustration personally, I submit the evidence:

"FIRMS PENALIZED FOR WAGE BOOSTS

"The Regional War Labor Board yesterday announced penalties against four firms, three in Philadelphia and one in Baltimore, for giving unauthorized wage increases to their employes.

"The firms were forbidden to charge off for income tax purposes sums ranging from $2,400 to $20,000.

"Alexander Frey, chairman of the RWLB Enforcement Division said that in each case 'laws governing the granting of wage increases set forth in the wage stabilization program were ignored.'

"The firms penalized and the amounts were:

S. Kind & Sons, jewelers, Broad and Chestnut Sts., $20,000, for increases granted starting in October, 1942, some of which subsequently were approved by the RWLB.

H-B Instrument Company, 2518 N. Broad St., $2,400 in settlement for wages totaling $9,999.99; reduction made because of extenuating circumstances.

S. Bogaslofsky, baker, 1914 67th Ave., $2,400, a compromise on total wages of $16,566.

Monument Printing Company, Baltimore, $15,000, for increases made since last February.

This "case" was "tried" by a panel of five men, from whose decision there was no appeal. The ordinary processes of civil law are all ignored and disregarded in such cases, and there is no safeguard or defense allowed or provided, to protect the rights of the "accused." Labor properly clamors for a just share in the prosperity it helps to create; if the employer agrees and co-operates he is penalized!

This technique of administering a government, whereby politics mean more than justice, and social theories supplant the laws of economics, has given rise to labor dictators who, in many cases, are stronger than the government! Ruthless men, seeing an opportunity to enrich themselves, have adopted "strong-arm" methods of legalized robbery, and hold up industry by labor prestige instead of the use of a gun! Consider this short news item:

"SHOWMAN SUES PETRILLO

"Manager of Theater Charges He was Forced to Hire Musicians

"New York, Jan. 29—(AP)—James C. Petrillo, president of the American Federation of Musicians (AFL) was a defendant with four others today in a $500,000 damage suit filed in Supreme Court here by a theatre manager who charged he was forced to employ union musicians against his will under threat of strikes.

"David T. Nederlander, general manager of Detroit's Lafayette Theatre charged that despite pleas that music was not required in the theater, which specialized in dramatic productions, it was forced "under duress and compulsion" to contract for six union musicians at a total weekly salary of $500 for a year."

Here is a clear case of legalized highway robbery! This business man is compelled to pay a tribute of six thousand dollars for the privilege of staying in business! The courts have consistently upheld the right of President Petrillo to use such methods, maintaining that under the present law "his union" can set the terms under which public commercialized music can be dispensed. It makes no difference that this particular theatre did not need, use, desire, or purvey music: if they did not "come across" they would face sympathy strikes from electricians, stage-hands, and all other organized labor forces, and be at war with the government of the United States!

Labor was under the impression that it had secured its own future and done a shrewd thing when it got control of Washington, but the fact is that trade unions were short-sighted when they vested their rights in politics and politicians instead of in constitutional law. They are beginning to learn that a Bureau which can oppress an employer can also turn and rend the employee! The White House sold its birthright for the pottage of political backing from the labor leaders: now it finds itself condemned by the very group it sought to placate! The breach gets wider by the month. Organized labor stands in a dangerous position today.

This is so for two reasons. First, it has created a Frankenstein monster that may some day destroy its creator! The following news item has some elements of rare humor in its contents, and the situation evoked much mirthful satisfaction when it occurred. The public, satiated with strikes and slowdowns, found something indescribably comical when members of the union employed union tactics *against* the Union! Following the accepted standard and pattern of conformity to legal procedure, the State Council of the CIO for Pennsylvania gave a "closed shop" contract to the five girls employed in the office of the Union, making them the "sole bargaining agency" with the employer, the C. I. O. The Secretary of the State Council of the C. I. O. attempted to fire his secretary, and the girls all staged a "sit-down" strike against the Union! Talk about a man biting a dog! The strike was denounced as "wild-cat"—"unauthorized"—"violation of union principles" and the girls faced stern disciplinary action, which may result in expulsion from the Union, and consequent loss of the right to earn a living! Read the details: noting especially the pitiful plant of the Union's president:

"GIRL STRIKERS OF CIO FACING UNION OUSTER

"The five office girls who work for the State CIO Council face expulsion from their union, the United Office and Professional Workers (CIO), and consequent loss of their jobs as a result of the wild-cat sit-down strike staged in the office last Tuesday, it was revealed Tuesday.

"The strike of those girls was unauthorized and violated union principles," said Olga Kane, president of Local 26, UOPWA (CIO). 'The publicity about that strike caused great harm and resulted in the loss of an election by the union.' The office girls were protesting attempts of Ben Probe, secretary of the State CIO Council, to fire his secretary, Mary Dupree. The sit-down ended when Probe and the girls agreed to arbitrate.

"Edith Vance, spokesman for the group, said they had been summoned to appear before a meeting of the executive board of the UOPWA (CIO) and had been told that disciplinary measures were contemplated.

"The UOPWA (CIO) has a closed shop contract with the State CIO Council."

A thousand employers chuckled with delight when they read that news. The CIO introduced the sit-down strike into American labor relations, now it is used against them by their own members! The indignation of the labor leader, who can't fire his own secretary, had been felt by them in thousands of cases where the union compelled them to retain incompetent help, and it was some small satisfaction to hear an officer of the union bellow when the shoe pinched *his* foot!

But there is a serious aspect to this issue also. By a strange coincidence, the same day these girls struck against their employer, the Union, fifty employees of the Continental Motor Company also staged a wild-cat strike.

"ATTEMPT TO SETTLE CONTINENTAL STRIKE

"Management-union conferences were being held Tuesday evening in an effort to settle a dispute which caused a wildcat strike of 50 employees of the Continental Motors Corp., and threatened to spread to other parts of the plant.

"The strikers, employees of the engine service repair department, refused to work Monday and Tuesday because of a controversy over classification on new jobs and a demand for pay increases. The strike was not authorized. Union officials were trying to get the men back to work."

When union members strike against the Union, stern repressive measures are resorted to and they are disciplined and punished. But when an equally unauthorized wildcat strike is conducted against an industrial employer, the strikers are coddled and petted, and wheedled into going back to work! Contrast the two episodes and the vastly different groups! How long can labor survive its own mistakes?

The second great danger to organized labor is the reaction of the armed forces to the selfish conduct of trade unions. To put it bluntly, the man in uniform is "fed up" with strikes and disputes, and is not loath to express himself in very strong terms whenever the issue comes up. Every correspondent who talks to fighting men has commented upon this, and my own correspondence and conversations with service men bear out this statement. In one of his last articles before his death, Raymond Clapper recounted a trip on a landing ship where

he talked with the commander and crew as they journeyed toward an objective. He told how they all gathered around
him for news from home, as they always do when a visitor
just from the States appears. He wrote: "We talked of strikes
and presidential politics, the only two public affairs subjects
that get into conversations out here, where every body is
absorbed in his duties and at other times is reading or wondering when he'll get home." He told how heated all service men
became when they talk about strikes, and to conclude the evidence fairly to Mr. Clapper, we quote his exact words to this
extent:

"John L. Lewis has become a symbol for this bitterness
among servicemen here, the same as I found him to be in
Africa and England last summer. His name is used as a
symbol for all the union leaders who put strikes above war
production.

Remember, these were not normally anti-labor men I
was talking with, but the run of the crew—farm boys and
workmen, some of them union members.

There were three union men in the group I chatted
with while going out to board this LST. Robert Toma,
Lorain, O., was a CIO welder at the American Bridge
Co. plant in Lorain. He said:

'I think what John Lewis is doing is close to treason.
I don't see how he gets away with it.'

Another was a member of the Typographical Union,
but did not wish to be identified, as he worked in a non-
union shop. He said he would like to see the Government
take over the railroads in order to end strike threats.

'We have to have unions,' he said. 'We can't let the big
corporations run things. But I'm against strikes.'

There was more about John Lewis from James C.
Jones, of Houston, Tex., of the AFL iron workers in the

shipyards. He said he was sure Roosevelt was the man for the place—speaking of the 1944 campaign. I asked him why the men felt that way. He said it was because Roosevelt was for the working man.

I don't know how it would add up if I could take a complete canvass, but everything I have found thus for is pro-Roosevelt and anti-strike.

One of the crew, named Gibson, was in the Navy before the war, and when his enlistment ran out in 1940 he took a job in an aircraft factory on the West Coast. In a short time a strike was pulled.

'I was disgusted, and I re-enlisted in the Navy,' Gibson said.

All the foregoing was said in the presence of a number of the crew, who acquiesced in what was said. They included James M. Lynch, Tenn., Anthony Matarazo, Mechanicsville, N. Y., John O'Donnell, Chicago; Victor Pelillo, the Bronx! John Healey, Fulton, Mo., and Ralph Snyder, Hardington, Neb."

Some time ago, one of the most famed members of the illustrious fighting force known as "The Flying Tigers" was speaking at a mass meeting in a large Texas city, and he concluded by offering to answer questions. One man asked, "What do the fighting men feel about strikes in war material plants?"

Instantly the answer came, "Personally, I'd shoot a striker as quickly as I would a Jap! Yes, even quicker, because the Japs are known to be our enemies, and the strikers are supposed to be our friends. But they are stabbing us in the back!" There was a burst of enthusiastic applause from the great crowd that showed the temper and trend of thought of the mass of America in terms that cannot be mistaken.

As for me, I would not go so far as this. If I had the authority, however, I would deal drastically with all strikes in war industries, but I trust fairly and with justice. The plan would be simple. If twenty-five thousand men engaged in making vital war material struck for any reason whatever, I would put them in uniform immediately, give them guns, and send them to some fighting front. Then I would bring back from that same combat area an equal number of tired veterans and put them in the jobs the strikers had voluntarily left. I am sure any fighting man, risking his life and suffering privation and discomfort, would gladly trade his fifty dollars a month in a fox-hole for a bench in a factory at fifty dollars a week!

There are of course two objections to this plan. The first is that green hands in the factories could not produce equipment efficiently or on schedule. Certainly not—but neither can skilled men while on strike! And in the case suggested, the men who would suffer from this reduced production would be the strikers who had gone to battle—which would be eminently fitting. Perhaps when they faced defeat because of lack of munitions these strikers would get some of the soldier's present point of view!

The second objection, however, is the real deterrent to my plan. If I did this, organized labor would gang up on me and vote me out of office! And that is a tragedy no true politician dares contemplate. I realize that these are plain words, but I only utter what millions are thinking. It is time somebody became vocal over the evils which threaten our unity and which delay victory. The great god Expediency is the only object of worship our political leaders recognize, and they lack the courage to run counter to millions of *organized* votes!

Let both labor and politics face this issue; when ten million ex-service men march home to demand an accounting, what alibis will they have to offer for this "double standard" which deals with soldiers on the basis of sacrifice, and with labor on the plane of politics? When men are battling for life in mud and cold or trembling with malaria in tropic heat; when soldiers are forced to halt an advance short of victory, or retreat from a hard-won position because supplies run short, it doesn't help to learn that the men who produce or transport these vital necessities are "on strike" for an extra dime an hour! I have heard many hundreds of men in uniform demand profanely, "Whose war is this, anyhow?" This attitude is reflected in the homes from which these lads departed, and labor is blind if it does not see the irreparable harm it is doing its own cause by its present conduct.

Remember also that these ten million men will come marching home some day, demanding jobs. How will the present set-up of union dominance of industry deal with this crisis? These men will be completely indifferent to jurisdictional questions. They want jobs! It will mean less than nothing to them that a certain group has become "sole bargaining agent" in their absence: work they want and work they will have! Beyond question, these men who fought for a free world will never pay tribute to the coffers of labor racketeers for the privilege of earning a living. Picket lines will never halt them: these are the lads who crashed through the "picket lines" of Fortress Europe and who smashed the lines of the Japanese Empire! Having fought foreign enemies to earn the right to live, they will not hesitate to battle domestic foes if the need arises; they will also fight for the right to a living. Deny or restrict that right and they will smash you ruthlessly, whether your leadership is in politics or in organized labor.

Some modern Paul Revere should arise in the ranks of the trade unions to sound the alarm, crying, "Wake up, labor, or perish!"

So while it is true that the Church cannot claim too strong a position in regard to organized labor, we are not the only group that needs to face an issue and take stock of our immediate future. Organized labor needs the Church as much as we need them! Future democracy will have no laurels for those who betrayed her under the guise of serving the working man, nor will she have any acclaim for a church which lost its vitality in an hour of desperate need. It looks as though the revival should be a double-barrelled affair since we are both at fault and need each other.

Consider labor's debt to Christianity, and see how logical and natural it would be for us to unite our forces. It can almost be put in one short sentence: *there are no labor unions in heathen lands!* Trade unions originated in Great Britain early in the 19th century, which was long after the translation of the Bible into the common speech, and was a direct dividend of the awakening Christian conscience. The movement was transplanted to the United States a generation later, and afterward spread to France, Germany, and other countries that had been enlightened by the philosophy and precepts of the Gospel. As far as I know, or have ever seen, or observed, there are no trade unions (in our conception of that word) in any Moslem country. And I know as a positive fact that such do not exist in any heathen culture. So trade unions owe their very origin to the enlightenment which comes in the wake of the preaching of the Cross of Christ.

Now note two strange facts. First; when a nation loses its faith, labor loses all of its gains through lack of restraint and tolerance. Before the debacle in France atheism had practically possessed that entire nation. The Catholic church, to which the largest number of religionists gave their allegiance, was formal, cold and dead. The Huguenots, who are historically the Protestants of France, had quit protesting and had lost their vitality. Only the small and struggling French

Baptist Church was manifesting any aggressive evangelism, and they were numerically few. They were aided to some extent by the Salvation Army, which also was too small to count for a great deal. The leaders of defeated France who survived the tragedy publicly stated that this was one of the major causes of the grim collapse. They laid equal blame on the labor unions which restricted production, paralyzed industry with strikes and arguments, and betrayed their own country into slavery. But most observers failed to note that the French labor organizations surrendered the restraints of faith before they blindly destroyed themselves. They selfishly fought for their own class interests and desperately preserved what they thought were "social gains". Now, under the Nazi heel they lost all, including honor, liberty, and the right to belong to a trade union!

The other point of equal significance is the fact that in Fascist countries labor unions are not permitted. Hitler and his Gestapo ruthlessly stamped them out in Germany as a preliminary to the enslavement of the nation. This condition was only possible, however, after the German Church became apostate to the true Gospel of Jesus Christ and had lost its own faith. We must never forget that modernism originated in Germany and that the false philosophy of organic evolution was spawned there as well. No race that loves God and His Son can exalt itself as a "super-race", or honestly believe they are destined to conquer and rule the earth by divine right!

In communistic Russia, governed by an equally brutal and despotic system, the only trade organizations allowed are those fostered and controlled by the State. In Russia under communism a modern labor leader like John L. Lewis would be shot the first time he dared express an opinion or formulate a demand. But Russia was dominated by atheism under Stalin: the historical example was faithfully followed there also. Smash *religion* first, then it is easy to enslave the populace in all other deportments of life.

Let labor make no mistake here: the Church of Christ is the bulwark behind which trade unions are fortressed and defended. If labor helps to demolish that defense, labor is doomed. So in facing the problem of survival in this age of change and reformation which approaches revolution, the destiny of labor is linked to Christ, the Church, and the Bible. The threads of our mutual fates are so inter-woven and entwined we need each other if either is to fulfill its purpose in the service of the race. Even as the Church has learned the wisdom of keeping separate Church and State, labor has to discover that governmental powers which can restrict capital can chain labor as well! For every "quid" labor gets from government, she must render a "quo"—and soon they are out of concessions! The unions of America have been playing with a two-edged sword, and they will be wise if they cast it aside.

We *can* help each other! But it will take honesty and effort on the part of both parties—it must be a truly-mutual aid pact. The organized Church would welcome a closer fellowship with organized labor. Can we heal the present breach?

We must for the benefit of both!

This is the chief modern crisis!

I recently discussed a great plan for a project that should be pressed to a complete and successful conclusion; an experiment that should be tried at once. The plan was under consideration by a Christian group in one of the great industrial centers of America. This company of devout Christians all felt the great necessity of forming a new liason with labor, and considered a simple technique to accomplish the goal locally. Their idea was to build and conduct a church of and for working people; one that operated primarily for the man in overalls. It was suggested that the new church be named, "The Church of Jesus Christ the Carpenter." The structure is to be of plain lumber—the seats will be comfortable benches of the tabernacle type; in place of a pulpit the platform will have a Galilean carpenter's bench, and the preacher will wear overalls instead of a frock coat! The entire plan is to emphasize the fact that our Lord and Saviour was a laboring man, as well as the Son of God. His chief invitation was "Come unto me *all ye that labor* and are heavy laden, and I will give you rest!" Any preacher would be proud to be pastor of a church like that! Such a church ought to illustrate the pattern of labor's future devoutness, and also be an example of the essential unity between Faith and Works!

Perhaps two alarm clocks are needed in the present situation—one to arouse labor to her peril and the other to awaken the church to the need of evangelism. The sad estrangement between the two organizations which owe so much to each other, would never have come to pass if we had been true to the redemptive Gospel and had continued in our ancient pattern of conduct. If we can again carry the Cross to the laboring masses, they in turn will carry the Cross with us to the redemption of our generation and the solution of our most difficult problems.

Extremists on each side will condemn me for this chapter; the fanatics of modernism will score me for honestly confessing the sad results of scholarly apostasy, and the rabid leaders of selfish labor groups will blast me for pointing out *their* faults. But I do not write for either of these groups: my words are rather an earnest plea to the vast, substantial, sane majority in both camps. The Church and the Unions should clasp hands and together build as much of stability and permanence into the immediate future as conditions will permit. Thus only can we survive the present crisis.

Chapter II

NATIONAL DEFENSE AND THE CHRISTIAN CONSCIENCE

THE second great crisis which faces the organized church in our times is the problem of war and our obligations, duties, and activities in defense of our country when it is endangered or invaded. It seems odd that such questions should ever arise; the natural impulse of every worthy citizen of any democracy would and should be to spring to the defense of his country in any hour of danger. But the modern leaders of organized Protestantism have lead us so far from the original form of our basic Revelation and have so distorted and colored the real teachings of Christianity that many Christians are honestly bewildered and confused by the Babel of modernism. The very meaning of such plain words as "duty" and "patriotism" have been changed and these terms perverted to false teachings that constitute treason in many cases. And the campaign has been waged in the name of Christianity. To this group of false prophets must be added the pernicious and vociferous educators who are imbued with such false ideals of internationalism as to be communistic in their instruction, and who are in complete revolt against nationalism or patriotism in any form. So deeply have these combined forces made inroads into our traditional love of country and eagerness to serve her, they have actually brought the organized church to a place where she must return to her old and former conception of duty, or be condemned and outcast by the very nation we should be proud to serve.

One of the most unusual scenes enacted in a modern court of law occurred recently in New York, when five young students of theology stood before the judge to receive a sentence for refusing to obey the law. With calm deliberation and after long thought, they had decided that the act of registering for selective service—even though they were clearly exempt from military duties—would violate the principles of the Christian religion, so they chose to go to jail rather than yield obedience to the law. The judge was deeply moved as he sought to reason with the group, sobs were heard all over the court room, and great publicity attended the affair.

The tragedy of the case is resident in the fact that the entire issue was so utterly needless. The students were martyrs to a flagrant mistake, or rather we should say they were the victims of an unfortunate choice in their system of education. The judge did his duty courageously, in spite of his natural reluctance to pass sentence, and every law abiding person in America should honor and commend him for his fidelity to his obligations. He had no choice in the matter, which is to be regretted. It would have been far better if the law had empowered the court to say to the five wilful lawbreakers:

"Young gentlemen, you have calmly decided that the United States of America are not worth defending, and that the American way of living is not worthy of any great sacrifice. The flag which you refuse to protect has guarded and shielded you from infancy, you have been educated at public expense, but now you hold that this government is not entitled to your aid in a time of crisis and need. You will therefore now choose the country in which you would rather live and the government you believe to be better than ours, and we, the people of the United States, will provide you with transportation to that place." This would have been justice, pure and simple, but the court was not allowed such discretion.

The principle upon which these young men stood was *not* Christianity. All the legitimate precepts and concepts of

Christianity are drawn from the New Testament, and that Book, properly read, does not teach pacifism. Supine surrender to wrong and evil are utterly foreign to all the teachings of Jesus Christ. If these young men had been following the instructions of Jesus, instead of being led by human teachers who deny the supreme authority of Christ and who are determined to replace His precepts and practices with a more "liberal theology," the entire incident would have been avoided. Their chief error was their early surrender to an un-Christian and anti-American philosophy. They studied in colleges where patriotism was derided and pacifism was enthroned, and passed on to a seminary which is noted for its advanced liberalism. The logical and natural end of such a course of instruction was reached before the bar of justice.

To help the young men of America to think their way through the fog of propaganda which pacifists have raised to obscure the problem of national defense, it is highly desirable that we offer them a clear record of the general Christian teaching concerning war and the defense of heath and hearth. There is nothing in the Christian religion which demands that its adherents shall be less worthy citizens than the man who has no faith! Quite the contrary. Christianity, properly understood, encourages the development of all that is worthy and noble in the individual, and patriotism is certainly not the least of such virtues.

So much depends on the point of view. I was reminded of this fact very effectively on a visit to the territory of Hawaii some time ago. In my preaching mission I went to many places, but the meeting which I enjoyed the most was a convocation held for the students at the Mid-Pacific Institute. All of the student body are of Oriental descent, this condition being a pre-requisite for admittance to the school. At the close of my address, I was surrounded by a company of boys of college age, all brown of skin and slant of eye, characteristically Japanese in appearance. They were all American citizens by virtue of their birth in the territory. We had a most interesting discussion which lasted a half-hour.

The session ended when I said to one of the lads, "I would like to ask a rather delicate question. In case of war with Japan, what would you boys do?" the answer was instantaneous: "Why, we would do like anybody else. We would fight!"

I wanted to ask, "On whose side would you fight?" but felt that the question had to be phrased diplomatically, so as to give no offense. But while I was still hesitating for the right words, another lad said most indignantly—"Of *course* we would fight! Those Japs have no right to come over here and take our country: let them stay home where they belong!"

There was a unanimous buzz of acclamation, and I went away somewhat surprised. But in a few minutes my surprise turned to pleasure, and I said to my companion, "Why not? My father came from Liverpool and my mother from Scotland. And if the British attempted invasion of the United States, I would be in the crowd which met them on the beach, armed with whatever weapon I could get. Those boys have the right to feel the same way. Their parents came from Japan, ours came from Europe, but we agree that *our* land is well worth defending."

The sincerity of this statement and the honest patriotism of these lads has been demonstrated forcefully since that interview, for with the base attack upon Pearl Harbor Japan invaded the United States, and we found ourselves at war, when we desire only peace. Now these boys are in uniform, American citizens and soldiers, serving their homeland with a fierce pride in their honored responsibility, and setting examples of devotion to our country which are not excelled by Americans of any other ancestral group.

In direct opposition to this point of view we have the modern philosophy of pacifism, a doctrine which demands absolute abstinence from forceful resistance to any evil. The bearing of arms in any cause is prohibited, even in the cause of self-defense, or the defense of the weak and oppressed. This teaching naturally results in the utter negation of patriotism.

Pacifism in America springs from two sources, the first of which is not germain to this present article, and which will therefore be dismissed with a few sentences. This is the type of pacifism which is pure propaganda, disseminated by certain communistic organizations which desired to handicap rearmament in America. Such groups as "The American League for Peace and Democracy," "The American League Against War and Fascism" (but not against Communism!) and kindred groups are purely subversive for political and ideological reasons, and America has learned to recognize them and their purpose.

Their propaganda was dictated solely by the necessity of following the Communistic Party Line, and of keeping their utterances in harmony with the orders and ideals of Moscow. That their interest in world peace was far from honest was established when these same leaders sought so desperately to get our government to intervene in the Spanish war and thus aid the hard-pressed Communists of Spain. It was further illumined by their silence and lack of condemnation of Stalin when the army of Russia marched into Poland to divide the spoil with Germany. Stranger still was the complete reversal of their advertized position when Hitler and Stalin made their short-lived compact of mutual trust and esteem, and gave guarantees to each other assuring the integrity of the territory of each nation. And when Germany invaded Russia, forgetting all of their previous platitudes concerning peace and non-resistance, they screamed for war in Russia's defense and protection! We therefore discount these pressure groups and political showhorses, and consider just the essential element in our present discussion.

The second and more serious type of pacifism comes from an earnest, but mistaken group of honest Christians, who are frankly bewildered and distressed by war's horrors and cost. They dream of a day when honor and unselfishness shall be the guiding principles of statesmen and rulers, and when no man will covet the wealth and territory of another. They hope by covenant and treaty honorably observed, to hasten the day when men shall beat their swords into pruning hooks and their spears into plow-shares, and shall study war no more. They seek a foundation for their vain hope in the Bible, and give to their philosophy a religious aspect which confuses the issue and brings a cry of persecution if they are opposed in this basic error.

Pacifism of this type is a more serious matter, as it is apt to become a definite handicap to national defense. If this school of thought multiplies until it represents the majority of our man power, and only the minority is left for active service, farewell to democracy and liberty! The government at present exempts such religious conscientious objectors to war from active service, but this custom could not be continued if pacifism became the general belief of the nation.

The propagators of this idea are generally men and women in strategic positions, such as school teachers, ministers, and writers. Their influence far exceeds their proportion to the population, and they may well weaken the morale of the potential fighting forces. Indeed, the process is well under way even now.

Yet these are dangerous and challenging days, when the forces of progress and decency should present a united front. The world is on fire, and we can't have the firemen quarreling over which hose we shall use, or how the nozzle shall be directed! It would be a major tragedy if our attempt to prepare our country for future defense should be hindered, especially by those who reason from a false premise.

The major thesis of all history may well be reduced to an axiom: "Aggression is only restricted by force of arms!" I do not know a single exception to that principle in all the records of human history. The combined voices of archeology and written history write to cry out to our generation, "They take who can, and they keep who may." All the loving kindness and brotherly love of which a race is capable, never stopped the hordes of Assyria when they were lusting for loot and conquest, and the same statement applies to every age. Fight or perish, is the only choice left to nations even in our century. Arms—and men capable of using them—are the only hope of a peace-loving people.

As an instance, we may compare the varied results met with by one conqueror of our day. The people of Korea were dedicated to non-resistance with a united religious fervor. When Japan invaded Korea, the people were true to this principle, and met the aggressor only with *passive resistance*. The result is a matter of history. There is now no Korea, but in its place a Japanese province, called Chosen.

The people of China are not warlike by nature or culture— they are belligerent only for defense. But since they were at least partially armed, and believed that no nation had the right to invade and oppress them, they rallied like heroes against the conqueror, and China is still a sovereign state. Her courage and fortitude have inspired the world, and have given us an example which we would do well to heed. They have also proved our conceded premise, that conquest and invasion can only be prevented by force of arms.

It is quite proper to raise the query, "Is the American way of life worth preserving?" There can be only one answer to that question. We do not claim to have the perfect government, and we admit that there is much room for improvement.

But having sojourned temporarily under every other form of government known to man in the present age, we can say of our own land—"With all our faults, I love us still!" I would not trade my citizenship, with its privileges *and* obligations, for citizenship in any other country on this globe. I saw a sticker on the wind-shield of an automobile a few days ago, which read, "America: Love It or Leave It!" To which I echoed a hearty "Amen."

I believe that most Americans feel just this way. We say that the form and substance of American life *is* worth preserving. Then it is legitimate to ask, "If that is so, why shouldn't *you* help to preserve it?"

To this query the pacifist replies, "Because my religion forbids me to bear arms."

There are two answers which could be made to that statement. The first one is in the form of a question: "What sort of religion permits its adherents to live under the defense and protection of a flag and government in times of peace, sharing in all the blessings and benefits of citizenship, but commands its devotees to refuse to aid that flag and government in a time of crisis and need?"

Certainly that base religion is *not* Christianity—and if it were, Christianity would be doomed, and would well deserve to be blotted out! But this is the attitude, not of orthodox Christians, but of the strange and subversive sects which masquerade under the name of Christ. Our constitution guarantees religious freedom and the right to worship to all citizens ,but it does *not* give the right to destroy the constitution or rebel against the government in the name of religion! One of the strangest of all hypocrisies is the hypocrisy of pacifism. First, you have noted how these sects all deny allegiance to the flag and government, but all of their members are eager to take jobs in government employ and live dependent upon the "wicked system" they so blatantly denounce!

Any job on the public payroll is acceptable to them, from school teacher to stenographer, or clerk in a draft board! They denounce the whole system of human government, and boldly state all such are actuated by Satan, but the moment their supposed "rights" are challenged they seek refuge under the strong arm of the law of the land, and run to the courts for protection!

One of the most pathetically humorous spectacles in our century is the eagerness of ordained ministers who stormed against preparedness and preached pacifism for a decade, hastening into a chaplain's uniform, accepting a commission, and receiving better financial compensation than they ever enjoyed before! These men offer a complete refutation of the propaganda they themselves bruited about for years, and illustrate clearly the pathetic poverty of honest intent in modern pacifism.

The most subversive and traitorous sect in the United States is not one of the many "Bunds" who parade under vari-colored shirts, but is the organization known as "Jehovah's Witnesses." They would be far more honest if they called themselves "Jehovah's *False* Witnesses" because their conduct and doctrine are alike contrary to the Word of God. They deny the deity of our Lord Jesus Christ, and claim a unitarian premise of faith in *one* God, not *three*. This one God, they say is Jehovah, and He has no fellow or other personality than Jehovah. He does not possess or require a mediator between man and Himself, and all men who wish can just worship Him and thus be saved. There is no need of a Saviour, and the claims of Jesus, Who said "I am the way, the truth, and the life, no man cometh unto the Father but by Me" are derided, rejected, and ridiculed. So they are *not* Christian: and since they repudiate the major portion of God's Word, they are certainly not true witnesses to Jehovah, Whose name is also "Jesus."

This entire sect is dedicated to treason, and in any other country than complacent America would be jailed or executed. They teach and advocate active resistance to the draft act, and maintain the false principle that every man in uniform is a servant of Satan. They refuse to have any part in any defense or war activity in any form whatever.

In this they differ from true conscientious objectors, such as the "Quakers" and Mennonites; all of whom have won the respect and admiration of the nation and of most of the world by their magnificent records of service and sacrifice. The grand story of the Units of the American Friends, who in the past formed ambulance corps, conducted reconstruction work and succored vast populations at their own expense is one to make the heart glow with pride in humanity. The courage and fortitude of these quiet heroes has never been exceeded, not even by the magnificent personnel of the famed R. A. F.— whose devotion to duty saved England in the days of the German supremacy in the air.

This has always been true of the Quakers. They serve when and how they may, short of actually bearing arms, and the world respects them for their accomplishments. It was the Quaker, Robert Morris, whose fortune was placed at the disposal of the struggling republic in the days of George Washington, who made it possible for the battle to go on to the point of victory.

And in that exact pattern the Mennonites have also manfully borne their share of the heat and burden of the struggles through which we have gone as a nation. Although their historic credal position forbids them to engage in battle, Mennonite bands have labored to build ships and provide the sinews of victory, even as Mennonite money has been placed at the disposal of our government as the need arose.

"For "pacifists" of this type we can have profound respect, even though we differ with their interpretation of a Christian's duty, but the "Jehovah's Witness" are quite different from these. They defy the law, and teach their children disrespect of the flag and the government whose protection they claim as a "constitutional privilege." And more—they have been engaged in a planned attempt to destroy the morale of our armed forces ever since we entered the war. Hitler has no more devoted helpers in this land than the volunteer aids of Jehovah's Witnesses, and if a tragedy should occur and he should win this war, he ought to honor every member of this traitorous sect with an Iron Cross!

Some few months after Pearl Harbor, I was called to Wrightstown, New Jersey, to open and direct a great service center of evangelistic work for the men of Fort Dix. Within a week of the time our center opened, the Jehovah Witness termites descended upon us. I was coming out of the gymnasium one night, where I had been boxing with some lads and leading them in some fun and exercise, when a sergeant stopped me in the hall and asked, "Doc, what sort of a joint are you people running here? Are you Americans, or Nazis?" Somewhat surprised I asked the sergeant what was bothering him, and he handed me a pamphlet saying, "One of your helpers just gave me this: he's passing them out to all the boys."

I took the leaflet, and saw to my surprise that it was a viscious assault upon every man in uniform. It frankly stated in the sight of God every soldier was a murderer, and would be condemned for the sin.

I said, "Sergeant, none of *my* helpers gave you this, we want to help the army; not hinder it. Where did you get this?"

He pointed to a big, husky man in the hall, and said, "He gave it to me."

I went up to the stranger and asked who he was, and what right he had to be distributing literature in our building. He replied that he was a Jehovah's Witness, and the constitution of the United States gave him the right to propagandize in any public place. He said if I didn't like it I could have him arrested, and in the meantime he would just stay and give out his tracts!

Very quietly I said, "No, you are wrong on all points. The constitution gives you no right to destroy the morale of the United States Army: this is *not* a public building, it's *my* building, and private property. I shall not have you arrested —I'll just give you thirty seconds to get out of here. If you don't, I shall beat you up and throw you out, then *you* can have *me* arrested!"

He was out in *twenty* seconds, and never came back again. I thus proved to my own satisfaction what I had long suspected, that their so-called "pacificism" is predicted upon physical cowardice, and they do not care to risk their own precious carcasses on a principle that could be defended!

In the vicinity of Army Camps all over the nation I have seen them at their insidious work of undermining the army: I have crossed the trail of their treachery at naval stations, and on the streets of my own home city their brazen women have accosted me frequently with treasonable utterances.

Among the Negroes of the Southern States their agitators have gone, and in both Texas and Louisiana I have known by direct testimony that they have counseled armed revolt by the Negroes against the whites, claiming that only by race war can the Negroes obtain economic justice. This, as much as any other act, manifests their hypocrisy. Professing to hold all armed force in abhorrence, they nevertheless seek to foment strife and bloodshed to suit their own evil purposes.

They are among the finest aids Tojo has in the land, and if Hirohito knows of their activities he must be greatly comforted thereby!

Only in America could such an organization of Traitors flourish: I would like to see them attempt these practices in Germany or Japan! Or even in Russia. This also illustrates their weird mentality: they work ceaselessly to destroy their only refuge. They are buttressed behind American liberty, but that freedom is now threatened and can be preserved only by military might. If our arms *should* fail, the "Jehovah's Witnesses would soon find themselves laboring in chains under the whips of Japanese taskmasters. And instead of aiding in the preservation of their own safety and freedom, they bore from within for the destruction of our common citadel.

The entire procedure of such pacifists constitutes a negation of all logic and reason. How can pacifists *resist* their own government, and still be true to their principles?

The philosophy certainly constitutes also a denial of God's Word, for the opening verses of the thirteenth chapter of Romans certainly enjoins service to the civil government! So the simple summary is that pacifism constitutes *double-barreled* treason! First to the government, which has a right to the aid of every citizen in times of stress and danger, and to refuse that aid *is* treason. Second, to Jesus Christ; for in order to justify his stand the pacifist has to ignore the Scriptures, repudiate the plain teachings of Christ concerning our clear duty, and thus bring His name into disrepute by wresting His teachings into a pattern He never intended them to portray.

All this, to my way of thinking, is the direct result of the repudiation of the Gospel of regeneration of the individual, which in turn is a natural result of the error of modernism. Since the claims Jesus made to deity are all denied by the leaders of liberalism, and since they do not believe that "Christ died for our sins, according to the Scriptures," quite naturally they are in revolt against orthodox Christian evangelism. With no message of salvation and redemption, the modernists were forced to find some other theme to expound, and they hit upon the popular and alluring suggestion of universal peace. They framed their own false premises and unwarranted conclusions in a pseudo, New Testament border, put their own interpretation on the word of Jesus, ignored or denied the authenticity of any Scriptures which were opposed to their fallacy, and emphasized pacifism as the major Christian message.

More than any other group in America, the modernistic leaders of Protestant Christianity were responsible for Pearl Harbor. The Methodist Church was the chief offender in the issue, maintaining a powerful political lobby whose business was to hamstring the navy and cripple the army through legislative pressure. Their conferences were devoted to deriding patriotism, and their schools advocated an internationalism which was based upon the spurious theory of the brotherhood of man which obsesses all modernists. Their bishops uttered criticisms of the government and condemnations of preparedness which are still bearing fruit in blood and death, and which helped to send raw recruits against skilled veterans on all the battle fields of the world. We entered war faced with the necessity of raising, equiping, training, and preparing an army and navy *after* the fighting had begun! A large share of the lives sacrificed in our early battles can be laid directly at the doors of the military leaders of pacifism, who are even now preparing to renew their campaign when the armistice is signed!

The second greatest offender in this matter was the mighty Presbyterian Church. The theories and technique of pacifism possessed the leaders of their governing bodies, and such iniquitous overtures as the "Cayuga Overture" which demanded that the constitution of the Church be changed to condemn any Presbyterian who took up arms to defend his country very nearly passed the Assembly. Had this been adopted it would have constituted a complete defiance of patriotism, and would have excluded from Presbyterian membership any man whose love of country impelled him to bear weapons in defense of it. And the leaders of this vicious campaign are but biding their time, waiting to repeat their efforts.

The organized church is going to have to face this issue shortly after the present war ends, and she will decide aright or go under, submerged by a popular storm of denunciation by the decent citizenry of America. It is a real crisis, and we must be prepared to meet it. In the post-war world, what shall the attitude of the Church of Christ be on the question of armed defense, preparedness, and military training?

I repeat the previous question: "What sort of religion permits its adherents to live under the defense and protection of a flag and government in times of peace, sharing in all the blessings and benefits of citizenship, but commands its devotees to refuse aid to that government in a time of crisis and need?"

To that religionist we can positively answer:

"Your religion is *not* new Testament Christianity!" Concerning this issue, the pacifist may be honestly mistaken, or misled. In any case I hope he will read and ponder these following words with an open, inquiring mind. I have a vast sympathy for those young men who feel torn between natural patriotism and what they conceive to be their religious duty, and I desire greatly to help them.

In any attempt to interpret the teachings of the Bible on any subject, there are certain rules which all honest exegetes know and follow. One is: "A conclusion must not be reached through an appeal to isolated or unusual texts, but the general content of the entire Revelation must be observed." The pacifist arrives at his conclusions in absolute violation of this rule. He wrests certain texts out of their context, and utterly ignores all others which do not support his preconceived conclusions. Instead of deriving his teachings *from* the Bible, he appeals to Holy Writ to bolster and support his prejudices. This is contrary to the accepted method of true Bible study.

The second rule to be observed is: "Difficult and ambiguous texts must be interpreted and understood in the light of parallel passages which are clear and explicit: the general trend of *all* references to decide the final meaning."

When we follow these sane and simple rules, we note some rather surprising facts about the Lord Jesus Christ. He was at least no "molly-voddle," and on certain occasions He was an apostle of direct action! He also could use strong terms of indignation as when he said to the Pharisees—"Oh generation of vipers! Who hath warned *you* to flee from the wrath to come?" These may sound like strange words from the lips of Him whom poets have called "Gentle Jesus, meek and mild," but it must be remembered that He was not always in that mood.

As far as pacifism is concerned, it seems to have been foreign to His nature. In His words we find no tirades against war, none of the modern inveighing against its cost and waste, and none of the polished platitudes which flow, without end, from modern orators on this theme. Indeed, as has been pointed out time and again, Jesus got along far better with Roman soldiers than He did with the venal priests of Israel!

Who can forget His conduct, when He saw the money changers, desecrating the temple of God with their unhallowed commerce? He made a whip of cords, and with fierce indignation He drove them out of the sacred precincts. Their tables He overturned and their persons He lashed, until they fled in fear. This was direct action with a vengeance. It was a clear case of righteous use of weapons, in that it was the whip which accomplished His purpose. The whip and the vigorous expenditure of manpower and muscle!

I know, as do you, the common attempt to discount the importance of this record. Pacifists tell us that Jesus did not use a real whip, but he twisted some small bits of string into a *symbolic* whip, and used it only as a badge of authority. This "interpretation" is contrary to fact, and is refuted by philology and psychology. The Greek word which St. John uses to define the "scourge of small cords" always means rope. The word is "schoinon" and refers to a rope made of bulrushes twisted together, like manila rope is made in modern times. The only other occurrence of the word in the New Testament is in the twenty-seventh chapter of Acts, and there it describes the anchor ropes which held the great ship in a storm. But the word is found frequently in ancient papyri, as for instance, in the Papyrus Oxyrinchus, III—502:36, where we read "The reel of the aforesaid, well provided with a new rope." It is needless to multiply instances, the clear statement of the gospel record is that Jesus made a scourge of small ropes, and with it he attacked the persons of the swindlers who polluted the house of prayer.

Note also the psychology of the action. St. John states that Jesus drove the money-changers out with His whip, and over-turned their tables, scattering their money all about. Let us remember that these money-changers were Jews of the lowest type. Their stock-in-trade consisted of cash, and they fled and left it behind! Do you think for one moment that such men would have been driven away from their money by a symbolic whip, made of grocer's string?

Nonsense!

That whip hurt; and Jesus plainly felt justified in using force to accomplish His righteous purpose.

Jesus not only recognized, but taught the principle "circumstances alter cases." Such an instance is plainly seen in Luke 22:36, where we read:

"And he said unto them, When I sent you without purse, and scrip, and shoes, lacked ye anything? And they said, Nothing. Then said he unto them, But now, he that hath a purse, let him take it, and likewise his scrip, and he that hath no sword, let him sell his garment and buy one."

One year and five months before he uttered these words, Jesus had sent the Twelve on a preaching tour of all the towns and villages of Israel. Since they went out to a friendly and hospitable country side, they were instructed to take no money, no knapsacks, or extra clothing, and to go unarmed. But after almost a year and a half the atmosphere had changed. Jesus and His teachings had been rejected, and the people had turned against Him. So now, sending the Twelve out into an antagonistic, enemy territory on their second preaching ministry, He ordered them to go prepared, and armed!

To apply this principle to a present issue, we might say that circumstances *still* alter cases! We can well afford to receive the young men of Japan with open arms and friendly hospitality when they come to join our student bodies, but when they come in uniforms, bearing machine guns and backed up by aircraft and artillery, a different reception is very much in order. In spite of lovely and roseate philosophies, common sense must prevail in actual circumstances. And Jesus recognized this fact, and so taught.

Pacifists do not consider His famous words, "I came not to send peace, but a sword!" The main object of Christianity is *not* to impart an undisturbed, serene, and placid life. The Christian is called to a warfare which is very real. St. Paul constantly likened the Christian to a soldier, and spoke of the spiritual conflict in military terms. It is not in vain that we have sung: "A charge to keep have I, a God to glorify: a priceless soul to save, and bring in triumph to the sky!" The church still chants, "The Son of God goes forth to war, a kingly crown to gain: His blood-red banner streams afar: Who follows in His train?" The Apostle Jude admonishes the Christian to "Fight for the faith once and forever delivered to the saints," and the entire concept of new Testament revelation is contrary to all that is inherent in pacifism.

A complete portrait of the Jesus of the New Testament demands that all the recorded details shall be incorporated in the finished picture, but pacifism leaves out more than it puts in! The book of Revelation closes the New Testament canon, and its theme is the return of Christ. This aspect of our Lord is not as Saviour, but as judge and King. So He is portrayed as a conqueror. Let us put together a few scattered verses, and read this description of Jesus:

Rev. 1:16 "and out of His mouth went a sharp, two-edged sword."

Rev. 2:12 "These things saith He that hath the sharp sword with two edges . . ."

Rev. 2:16 "Repent, or else I will come unto thee quickly, and will fight against thee with the sword of my mouth."

Rev. 19:15 (after the description of Christ returning to earth, leading the army of Heaven) "and out of His mouth went a sharp sword, and with it he shall smite the nations, and He shall rule them with a rod of iron and He treadeth the wine-press of the fierceness and wrath of God Almighty."

At once the cry goes up, "But this is figurative language!" Of course it is, that is self-evident. But *figurative of what?* The sword can't be taken as a symbol of love and peace, or of anything but battle, strife and conquest. So there are two sides to the New Testament portrait of Jesus. He *is* a Savior, loving and self-sacrificing in that aspect of His work. But He is also a conqueror, who shall subdue evil finally by the word of His power.

The thousand year reign of Christ is indeed to be a millenium of peace, but it also ends in war! In that last battle the arch-angel Michael is a general, and if angels are sometimes called upon to fight evil, why not Christians also?"

This is an academic question, however, and we can settle the subject of war and the Christian conscience by a direct appeal to the practical teachings of Jesus. The first of His utterances we shall consider is the famed statement, "Render unto Caesar the things that are Caesar's and to God the things that are God's." (Mark 12:17).

Since Jesus lived under the power and government of the Roman Empire, it is conceded that "Caesar" can be literally construed to mean the King, ruler, or group which has the right to rule a land. In this case of St. Mark's record, Caesar was the emperor, and he had two recognized rights. One was the power to tax his realm to support his rule, the other was the power to conscript his man-power to defend his realm. Those two rights are still recognized as being resident in constituted government today. Thus Jesus taught that any form of government which Christians could legitimately support by the paying of taxes, could also expect to receive their physical support if it was threatened by invasion. After all, what difference is there in the final analysis, between *paying* for a war, and participating in one?

This teaching, of course, does not apply to a war of aggression and conquest. I would die gladly to defend my native land from invasion. I would also die before I would wrongfully invade another country. There is no power so strong, no torture so fierce, that it could compel me to bomb and machine-gun helpless civilians, all for the aggrandizement of my own land. But if an invader assails *my* shores, he can expect to find at least one Christian soldier ready to repel him by force of arms.

The arguments for pacifism, drawn from the Christian sources, will not stand up under a simple examination. We often hear Matthew 26:52 quoted as an argument that Christians cannot render military service. Here we read:

"Then said Jesus unto Him, put up again thy sword into his place, for all they that take the sword shall perish with the sword."

Since this is offered as a general prohibition against any and all military service, to the confusion of many young men, perhaps it will help some if we analyze and consider the verse.

In the first place, it is primarily a warning against the use of carnal weapons in spiritual conflicts. We must remember that Jesus was facing the Cross, by which means He was to save such men as should later believe in Him. The purpose of Calvary could only be achieved by His voluntary and vicarious death, therefore He went gladly to that ordeal. His battle was with Satan, against the hosts of spiritual wickedness, and a carnal weapon was useless in that strife. He told Peter that twelve legions of angels awaited His commands, if He needed help—but went on to the victory alone. In a word, it is not by the armed might of marching men that the Kingdom of God is to finally prevail.

The statement, however, is not to be wrested into a complete and absolute prohibition of weapons where such are legitimately required. It is right and proper that police should bear arms, or none of us would be safe in bed or able to walk abroad by night. If the specific order to Peter is of universal application, how can His further words be true: "All they which take the sword, shall perish by the sword?" If an invader is not to be resisted by armed force ,how is he then to "perish by the sword"?

So this statement of Jesus cannot be intended to apply to proper defense. General George Washington took up the sword, and did so with the manifest blessing of God upon his subsequent conduct.

Abraham Lincoln was forced to the use of lethal weapons to defend the union.

China is battling even now for the very right of existence as a free nation.

Great Britain is writing one of the most magnificent chapters of all history by her courage and steadfastness in the face of appalling losses, and none who possess any semblance of logic would argue that it is her Christian duty to surrender in supine submission to her foes.

We believe that this text is simply a warning that they who depend on force to effect their desires will find it a weapon which will recoil against the user, if armed might is exercised in the wrong manner and cause. The revolt of a conquered people, for instance, always occurs at the most embarrassing moment for the conqueror! I am sure that the conquered Albanians were no very great help to the legions of Mussolini in the later conflict with Greece! Every new success of Hitler increases by just that much his future trouble and danger. It will soon absorb so much of his time and might to keep his conquered subjects quiet that he will be unable to grasp more and newer regions. And some day the very mass that he believes subdued will rise and rend him.

It has been so of every conqueror in antiquity, and will prove so again. But we would emphasize the fact that invasion and aggression are always defeated ultimately by armed, determined, efficient defenders. There is no other way to halt conquest than by an appeal to superior arms.

We conclude, then, that the admonition to Peter was directed against the *wrong use* of the sword, not against the sword itself. Many of our own religious liberties were obtained for us by the sword, and by the ability of Christian men to use it.

A second common argument for pacifism is argued from the next statement of Jesus, "Love your enemies!" To this principle we offer no rebuttal. I have no personal animosity toward any man. There is not a living man whom I hate. Certainly, I have enemies, no man could be active in the cause of Christ for twenty-five years and not make foes.

Atheistic societies have publicized their hatred for me; I have been sued for believing the Bible, calumny and bitterness have been heaped upon me. None of this has affected my attitude toward my fellow men, and I am sorry for such as have soured their days by hatred and unkindness. But this does not mean that I have cringed like a dog before my detractors; I have given them both barrels whenever they have carried the battle to me! And my religion does not condemn me for this. Quite the contrary. I have the commendation of the Sacred Scriptures when I *fight* for my faith!

"Love your enemies" is not a commandment issued to rulers and nations, compelling them to grovel before oppressors and supinely enter into slavery. On the contrary—we do not manifest true love when we allow evil to run unchecked, and a good, brisk spanking may ultimately manifest more love than a cowardly refusal to meet an issue.

The same holds true of the plea of pacifism, that God has said, "Thou shalt not kill." We accept that divine dictum, and abide by it. But the same God said, "Whoso sheddeth man's blood, by man shall his blood be shed!" How shall we reconcile these apparently conflicting laws? By the specific command of God, certain crimes against the community are to be punished by death. But the *individual* is not to take this law into his own hands, and slay for private vengeance.

The State does possess the power of punishment. In the Commonwealth of Israel this power was exercised by the people, and criminals who were condemned to death were stoned. In modern society this is not feasible, so the State delegates this power to an official, such as a sheriff or warden. So while this official acts to carry out the sentence of a court, he is not violating the commandment against personal vengeance. Rather he is obeying the commandment which orders that the murderer shall die for his crime. Acting in this capacity, he *is* the State.

In that same respect, soldiers are also the State. They are set for the defense of the land and its inhabitants, and are thus exercising a delegated power which is resident in the very principle of human government. The problem very naturally arises, "where shall this defense begin?" One man says, "on the beach, guarding our own territory." This, however, is not sensible. If we allow the enemy to get a foot hold on our soil, where multiplicity of fire power will help him, we might as well not fight!

So another man says, "meet him three miles out at sea!" Here again we run into difficulties. The armed ships of his convoy can shell our coasts at a range of twenty-five miles, and his armored craft can force a landing. If we meet him 50 miles out his airplanes can harry our cities, so why not stop him at a range of 250 miles? Or if it is possible, stop him 2500 miles away, at his very point of departure.

God has set soldiers as ministers of defense, let us leave this problem to experts and concern ourselves only with the question of the individual Christian conscience as it must meet the issue of national defense. To guide our decisions here, there are certain basic principles set forth in the New Testament. These may be summarized in a short and easy fashion.

First, Christianity should not and does not weaken patriotic obligations. On the contrary, a Christian should be a far better citizen than an unbeliever, as his perceptions are quickened by divine illumination and guidance. Secondly, Christianity enjoins and enhances obedience to constituted government in government's proper sphere. Beyond question this sphere includes defense of the realm. That such obedience to lawful authority is indeed a Christian duty, may be seen from such New Testament passages as these:

I Timothy 2:1, 2: "I exhort therefore, first of all, that supplications, prayers, intercessions, thanksgivings, be made for all men; for kings and all that are in high places; that we may lead a tranquil and quiet life in all godliness and gravity."

I Peter 2:13-17: "Be subject to every ordinance of man for the Lord's sake; whether to the king, as supreme, or unto governors, as sent by him for vengeance on evil-doers and for praise to them that do well. For so is the will of God . . . Honor all men. Love the brotherhood. Fear God. Honor the king."

Following this basic philosophy, some great Christians have added to the military annals of many lands, as generals, captains and privates and have sacrificed personal preferences to the need of the nation in time of crisis.

I am sure that back of much of the past outcry against national defense, there was the specter of parental fear that harm, or even death, may come to our sons because of military training. I think the opposite is more apt to result. War is a specialized business in our generation, and it is conducted by specialists. A man's chances at survival are in exact proportion to his knowledge of the technique of warfare. Untrained troops would have as much chance for survival and victory as a team of grammar-school boys would have in a foot-ball game with the Green Bay Packers!

There *are* some things worth dying for! The Chinese think that China is one of those things. The Czechs, the Poles, the Finns, the Lowlanders, also believed their lands were worth defending, and their liberties more to be prized than life itself. France, betrayed, in chains, now regrets the fact that she also did not persevere to the death!

What have these nations that we cannot claim? All of their liberties and splendors we possess to a greater degree. We have more that is worth defending than any other people on the face of this earth.

Christians know *how* to die! That fact is written in flames and blood on the pages of the past. We have died for our faith and for our lands, and if either are threatened we will write the same record anew.

I am a Christian, a minister of the gospel, and a believer in the Jesus of the New Testament.

I am also an American. To her defense I would pledge anew my life, my family, and if need be, my blood. And in so doing I would have the full consent of my Christian conscience, and the authoritative approval of the Christian Scriptures.

This has been the authoritative position of the organized Protestant Church of Christ from the very hour of our origin, and it has been the consensus of Christian agreement since the days of the apostles. Here is an issue we must soon face, a crisis to be weathered. In the post-war era, will we persist in our historical, logical, Scriptural, Christian, and patriotic philosophy of defense by armed force if need be, or will we be lead astray by wolves in sheep's clothing, chanting "another gospel," called pacifism? Our very survival may depend upon the answer to that question.

Chapter III

THE HOPE OF A LASTING PEACE

THE third great crisis which faces our forces today is the grave problem of future armed conflicts and the bright aspirations for a generation of peace which fill the minds of men even now. The crash of bombs and the shuddering rumble of heavy artillery is a weird diapason to have as an accomplishment to the song of a dove; but men, seeking release from reality and searching for some mental and spiritual haven for their wearied souls have adopted a natural defense mechanism in this peace propaganda. If we cannot have peace *now*, the next best thing is to dream of it as a possibility in the near future! So in place of a calm, honest, and realistic survey that would help us chart a sensible and practical course in the troubled days that lie ahead, we are being fed rosy pictures of a bright Tomorrow wherein dwelleth every good thing, and in which the evils of war will be unknown! We are also promised a stable world with complete freedom, liberty, justice, and economic security for all of the races of the earth: all of which is to be realized by turning the world's affairs over to the men whose past bunglings have brought us to our present sad condition. We have heard these siren songs of this perfect Tomorrow before, and have also been lead from the stern hard path of duty by the sweetness of these baseless promises, to our present distress and undoing. Men forget that "Today" *is* the "Bright Tomorrow" which starry-eyed dreamers promised us "Yesterday!"

The convenient shortness of man's memory is one of the chief assets of the politician, whether national or international in his sphere and scope of operations. Thus he can ignore the fact that all of the promises and hopes now held out to a war-wearied world are identical with those made in the same conditions in the years between 1914 and 1918! Only the slogans are changed—the contents of the promises remain the same. Then it was "This is the war that shall end war!" Now it is a war "To assure a better world to our children!" In 1918 it was the fashion to believe that "Territorial justice to the minority groups and smaller nations will ensure peace in Europe:" but now we profess to believe that "Economic equality and justice guaranteed to all people will remove the cause of war." After 1918 the philosophy of peace was to be realized through the technique of dis-armament: in our day it is to be achieved by forming a super-state that will enforce its dicta by the limited power of its combined arms. Wilson's "14 Points" have given place to the "Atlantic Charter" and the "League of Nations" has its successor in "World Government:" but the same mirages dance across the same desert landscape, and all are made of the substance of illusion.

All such promises are without foundation: we cannot assure peace for the next generation: They in their own day will determine the sort of a world in which they shall live, and circumstances and forces which we cannot foresee will be the basis of their decisions. All these glittering promises are baseless, primarily because they are made by politicians and not by statesmen: they emanate from the fertile imaginations of the architects of social theories. And since these visionaries ignore facts and despise the proved laws of sane economics, their words have no more worth than promises written in dust on a windy day. These great ideals are not intended to bear fruit, however; they are but the propaganda by which political schemers hope to perpetuate themselves in office.

The situation constitutes a crisis for the organized forces of Christianity, to the exact extent that we allow ourselves to be deceived by these false prophets and to the extent that we allow ourselves to become entangled in their visionary dreams. The danger lies in the fact that many of our most prominent Protestant leaders are among the very wildest of these extremists: having no gospel which contains any spiritual power, they fain would ensnare the Church into world planning. Thus they would lure us to the ancient error of Esau, and if we listen to them we will exchange our birthright as contained in the Great Commission which our Saviour gave to us, for the pitiful mess of pottage described under the impressive title of "The New World Order."

We may as well strip the scales of wishful thinking from our eyes and realize that there is no hope or assurance of a generation of peace to follow this war. We are unquestionably faced with a succession of future wars just as we have experienced a parade of armed conflicts in the past, and in all the empty schemes and suggestions emanating from deceitful politicians and modernistic church leaders alike, there has not been one sane or practical suggestion that would bring a whole era of peace.

Certainly the "Atlantic Charter" will not and cannot do so. It was a great ideal, but is doomed to failure because of certain basis weaknesses inherent in the document and common to frail humanity. Perhaps the greatest of the Charter's shortcomings is the fact that the Atlantic Charter was drawn up for the benefit of the Anglo-Saxon race alone! Its conditions were never intended to apply to China, although she is one of the greatest of the allied nations. She has certainly borne more of the heat of conflict and suffered greater losses to date than any of the other members of the United Nations; but who is naive enough to believe that Great Britain and the United States ever intended to divide the spoils with her on the basis of proportionate claims based on amount of suffering borne, or to fight for the interests of China where they clash with those of the British Empire? The conditions of the formed Charter certainly do not apply to the teeming masses of backward India, whose people will pose one of the gravest post-war problems the allies shall have to face. This document was not intended to benefit the defeated enemies with whom we are now at war: but they are the very folks who will *start* the next conflict! The victors will be quite content to rest upon their laurels for a generation: the vanquished will never rest content until they force the issue again in the hope of greater success in a return engagement!

The greatest weakness of the Atlantic Charter is the fact that it was simply a unilateral agreement between Great Britain and the United States. It was a beautiful dream put into writing by Prime Minister Churchill and President Roosevelt: but it ignored Marshall Stalin; he wasn't even there! And you just can't leave Joseph Stalin out of the plans for a future world; he won't be ignored! He also has some ideas of his own. When these great pronouncements were uttered by the rulers of the Anglo-Saxon race they were based upon the *presumption* that a victorious combination, the United States and Great Britain, would be free to impose their benevolent ideas upon all of Europe. But since then the picture has changed to a startling extent. The astonishing victories of this war have all been won by Russia so far, and her spectacular successes have given her a dominant position which has upset all previous bases of calculation. Victorious Russia has publicly, frankly and honestly stated her war aims, and has plainly declared that she has certain territorial aims which she intends to achieve before she lays down her arms. And the very territory Russia is so grimly determined to seize and retain lies within the sphere of influence of the Atlantic Charter! The frankness of Russia is to be commended regardless of what we may think of her purposes and ambitions, and it is refreshing by contrast, to the devious and impractical dreams which are all we hear from our own leaders!

The issue came into the open when the Polish government in exile challenged Russia over the question of the post-war border between the two countries. Russia not only stated her intention of re-establishing the old Curzon line as her boundary, but also enlarged upon her other aspirations. What ever transpires we cannot express surprise or claim ignorance of Russia's future actions, for even if they upset world peace, she has given clear warning of her intentions. And in the face of this announcement we must either revise or junk the Atlantic Charter, or prepare for another five years of war.

Let us make a short resume of Russia's aims, claims, and purposes, so that we can calmly consider our own future place in the picture and evaluate properly the wild promises of a future peace based upon equality and justice for the "smaller nations" in whose cause we claim to be so vitally interested.

Russia's first demand is that she secure from Finland certain sections of that country, to wit: (a) A small slice of North East Finland near Petsamo, which Russia needs to guard the flank of her important port of Murmansk. Without this region near Petsamo in her possession, the Russian government will always face the prospect of a surprise attack upon her chief arctic port. Then she also wants (b) the area of Kuolajaervi, and (c) the shore and territory surrounding Lake Ladoga.

The strategic reasons for this claim are obvious. Lake Ladoga is the largest lake in Europe, lying in extreme southeast Finland and northwest Russia. It has an area of seven thousand square miles, and its shores come perilously close to Leningrad. A hostile expedition which originated anywhere in Finnish territory on the shore of Lake Ladoga would constitute a serious threat to the safety of Leningrad, and it was to remove this danger that Russia went to war against Finland in 1939. At that early date the practical and wide-awake Stalin knew evidently that his dear friend and bosom companion Hitler was planning a double-cross and was going to invade Russia. His mistake was in under-estimating the strength of Finland. The Finnish army had been trained by German military experts and her famed Mannerheim Line had been constructed under the supervision of German army engineers. The Russians sent some raw recruits against the Finns whom, they thought, would profit by the training experience. They were poorly equipped and lacking proper artillery and mechanized aid. The awakening was rude and violent, and Russia suddenly found herself humiliated and defeated. The skilled and able General Timoshenko was put in command, and he spent six months training and drilling his forces in readiness for a determined assault.

The League of Nations expelled the Soviet Republic from membership because of this attack, but Stalin knew that the League was a dead issue, powerless and impotent, and the threat to his flanks was very vital and real. Early in 1940 the war machine so skillfully prepared by Timoshenko got to rolling, and the defeated Finns were forced to agree to the concessions demanded by the Russians. The strategic points thus secured saved Leningrad when the Germans invaded Russia, and from a pragmatic viewpoint Stalin was amply justified in his course. But the incensed Finns then joined with the apparently victorious Germans, hoping thus to regain their lost territory. Time has proved this to have been a tragic error, and the Finns face humiliating terms of surrender as these lines are written. And Russia is quite determined to retain these important points for her future defense, so Finland can count the loss as an accomplished fact. World opinion did not move the Russian dictator when he decided he needed these sections, and certainly no document like the

Atlantic Charter will compel him to return them when the war ends!

In addition to this slice of Finland, Stalin also announces that Russia will demand, take, and hold (1) All of Estonia, which has an area of 18,353 square miles, and which has been a "republic" in the Russian Soviet Union since 1921; (2) All of Latvia, with its area of 25,390 square miles, which country has been occupied by Russian forces since June 1940; (3) The entire territory of Lithuania, comprising 22,395 square miles; (4) the section of Poland East of the "Curzon Line;" (5) The Great Province of Bessarabia; all of which lands now lie under the mighty paw of the Russian Bear. And to lift that paw the other allies will have to slay or cripple the Bear!

So now we take a frank and honest look at the question under discussion, namely; the prospect of lasting peace when Germany and Japan are defeated. Calmly and without any thought of retreat, Russia stands over the spoils of war in the Baltic region, and says she will not give them up. The other allies will either consent to this acquisition with such face-saving grace as they can contrive, or fight Russia! So our choice here is very simple: we can repudiate the high ideals of the noble document called the Atlantic Charter, or we can wage another war! In any case, we should be realistic enough to answer the question which arises from such a choice: "In this pragmatic age, which of these two courses of action do *you* think the Anglo-Saxon nations will choose to follow?" My answer is that in the light of reality, said Atlantic Charter is even now as dead as the extinct dodo!

It would pay the average reader to do about six months research reading into the historical background of this situation, and see that Russia has much justification for her present demands. The more you know about the origin of these claims and the history of those countries the more sympathy you have for Stalin's position. It is not true that the present mess in the Baltic States springs out of the Treaty of Versailles; the roots go far deeper than that. The genesis of the matter goes back to the Polish wars of Conquest in the years between 966 and 1506 A. D. Our present sympathies are with the Poles as an aggrieved and persecuted people, but there was a time in history when Poland was a mighty aggressor nation, which came close to conquering the world in her day of power. The real source of all of this present trouble is in those ancient wars, and the divisions of territory which followed them. In a sense, the Poles are just reaping what they once sowed. Objects of sympathy now that adversity has come upon them, they were once hated and feared, as the Axis powers are hated and feared in Europe today.

Beginning with the wresting of vast territory from the great but feeble and tottering Moravian Empire, Poland pushed her conquests until she had subdued and enslaved all of her neighboring countries. Further, she did what Hitler failed to accomplish, she held on to her conquered lands and fastened the yoke upon the peoples thereof for many centuries. She took from Moravia all the great area from the Carpathian Mountains to the Bug River in her earlier aggressions, and by the year 1205 the mighty king and shrewd General Boleslaus had incorporated into his kingdom all the territory from the Baltic to the Carpathians, and from the Elbe River to the Bug.

No country or coalition could stand against the advance of the Poles, who ruthlessly subdued and added to their domain every rich land that they coveted. Before the end of the thirteenth century their flag flew over Galicia, Silesia, Livonia, Prussia, all of the Ukraine and a vast section of Red Russia. So Germany and Russia were the chief sufferers among the greater races, but all of the smaller peoples were swallowed up and sternly repressed. Nationalism smoldered beneath the surface in all these conquered and enslaved peoples, but they were too weak to make an issue of their intense desire for freedom and recognition. The only strong people the Poles could not defeat were the once-mighty Lithuanians, between the two peoples; and when the pagan Lithuanian Gagiello embraced Catholicism, he was crowned king of Poland under the name of Wladislaus II. From this time on to the period know as the Great Partition, the Polish-Lithuanian Empire had its heel upon the necks of all of its neighbors.

The Knights of the Teutonic Order was one of the three great military organizations that developed from the Crusades, and like their fellows they began as a charitable organization, developed into a military group, and finished as a chartered company of mercenary warriors who owned great estates and exercised rights of sovereignty over large sections of troubled Europe. In the 13th century, Bishop Christian of Prussia invited the Knights to aid in the military subjection of the Prussian heathen, and the Order became established along the border of Prussia. This brought them in sharp conflict with Poland, and for the most of a century the Knights fought to win back the Teutonic lands which the Poles had conquered. This conflict ended in the Peace of Thorn in 1466, which gave West Prussia to Poland and East Prussia to the Knights. By the terms of this treaty Prussia became a Polish province and Poland obtained a sea port and a seaboard.

The Poles came to the inevitable hour of retribution in the last quarter of the eighteenth century. They learned what all conquerors find out, that what is won by the sword may also be lost that way.

Catherine II of Russia, and Frederick II, King of Prussia united their forces because of common interests and in time brought about the destruction of Poland. At that time Poland had a population of eleven and a half million, a million of whom were Protestants or Greek Catholics. This minority had no civil or religious rights, and after the unchanging policy in any country overwhelmingly Roman Catholic, they were bitterly repressed. The emissary of Catherine demanded equality for this religious minority. This introduced a period of strife and armed conflict at the close of which Russia was garrisoning Poland and Poland was divided up between Prussia, Austria, and Russia; leaving Poland a small country with less than one third its former area, and a population of about three and a half million. This was the condition of that once proud but now unhappy land between 1793 and 1796, in which latter year the final partition was made. At that time Austria received Western Galicia and Southern Masovia while Prussia took Western Masovia with Warsaw; Russia taking all of the balance. Thus Poland passed out of history as a nation, until the rehabilitation of the Republic as a result of the Peace of 1918.

After the defeat of the Central Powers, the Polish question became a paramount issue. The Allies, following the high ideals of Woodrow Wilson's "fourteen points" were pledged to the freedom and political sovereignty of minority European races, and Poland was established as a republic. A large section of the new nation necessarily had to be taken back from Russia (who had taken it back from the Poles, who had previously taken it from them!) and the question of boundary became a formidable issue. An allied commission, headed by Lord Curzon, studied the situation and worked until they arrived at what seemed to be a fair and equitable decision. Incidently, the Allied Powers were singularly wise in their choice of Lord Curzon to head this mission. He was an authority on races and geography, had traveled widely in Asia and Baltic Europe, was a gold medallist in geography and had the necessary background to understand the involved problems his commission faced. The boundary they recommended followed an ethnographical line, and the Allied Powers accepted it and made it legal.

But Poland objected, and demanded more territory out of Russia, and took up arms to enforce her claims. The Bolshevik regime was embroiled with practically all of its border neighbors at the time, was torn by internal strife and dissent, and the Red Army was tired of war, and reluctant to carry on. The Poles pressed the campaign with valor and decision, forced the Russians to surrender the territory that Poland claimed, and set her own boundary. Russia ratified the military decision in a peace treaty, and Poland entered into possession of the lands thus won by force of arms.

In 1939 Hitler invaded Poland, and swept on toward Warsaw. At once Stalin threw his army into the Eastern portion of Poland to occupy what *he* called "Russian Territory" and to protect and preserve it from German conquest. He sincerely believed he was merely safeguarding the rights and interests of Russia: and I believe that history will support his claim. His present offer to the Poles seems moderate in the light of the past: he offers to set the Russian-Polish border at the agreed "Curzon Line" (which the Allied Powers once agreed was a just and fair premise) and to re-establish the boundaries as they were when Poland upset them by force of arms. Stalin quaintly believes that what a nation lost in military defeat she may justly regain by military victory! And to compensate Poland for this loss of Eastern land he offers to give her a large slice out of Prussia!

Personally, I think that is a grand idea! That portion of Prussia which Poland would thus receive was once under the Polish flag, she having conquered and annexed it in her early wars. Of course, if Germany wins this war there will *be* no Poland, and the government in exile should remember that. If Germany loses this war, the valor and sacrifice of the Russians will be a major contributing factor, and the Poles should also bear that in mind. The Germans, of course, will raise a bitter outcry if Prussia is carved up and divided among the victors, but since this is just what she planned for Poland, why should she object to a dose of *her own medicine?*

I introduce this issue here to show the blindness, the ignorance, and the utter folly of those who talk about a "lasting peace" to follow this present war! The question before our nation can be put in a simple sentence: "Shall American blood be shed to settle European border questions that have continued for hundreds of years?" I leave the answer to you! The issues have been fought over for many centuries: how can we talk of a "lasting peace" until such an irritating cause of war is removed? And how shall it be dealt with? If the decision of the peace council favors Poland, Russia will fight. She will only be following the example set by Poland after the decision of the Curzon Commission, when the Poles refused to abide by the award of arbitration. If the Council gives Russia what she has the historical right to demand, and the armed force to take, then Poland will have a grievance that may lead to a new war. If Prussia is divided, the Germans will never rest until they make an effort to win it back by battle—and the statesmen who plan for a peaceful future without facing these issues and solving them are mentally blind!

There are so many possibilities for war in the Baltic states alone that peace seems an impossible dream. Then when we add to these the further issues that center in the Balkan states, our hopes for peace grow even more dim. These two regions constitute a threat to the future which cannot be ignored. So important are they that they must be considered separately, as they pose entirely different problems. Of course, in a book as condensed as this one neither section can be fully discussed, but enough can be stated to show the utter and blind folly of talking about permanent or lasting peace while these questions remain unsolved. Russia, naturally, is the great source of future trouble, as she will never rest content until she has regained all that she considers hers and is in complete control of both sections.

To show the strength and justice of the Russian claims in the Baltic states, consider as a "case history" the ancient land called ESTONIA. Her history goes well back into old European wars, as she first enters the record through her early wars with the conquering Danish kings. The Estonians were a turbulent and fighting people, closely related to the Finns, whom they also resemble physically.

In the year 1219 A. D. the Danish conqueror Waldemar II made war on them, and for a base of operations founded the present city of REVAL, the capitol of Estonia, which is also called TALLINN. The town was first a military base, then became the center of an episcopal see, and has had a stirring history. The first Danish settlement was made there in 1093, but its prominence dates from the campaigns of Waldemar II. From it he conquered all of Northern Estonia, and in spite of incessant rebellion he maintained his grip on the region and passed it on to his successors. The Livonian Knights captured it in 1228, but the Danes won it back again in 1237. It was the center of battle between Danes and Estonian rebels until 1346, when the Danish king Waldemar III sold all of his Estonian holdings to the Teutonic Knights, who had previously conquered the southern half of the country. For the next three hundred years the Estonians were the serfs and chattels of their Germanic landlords and masters. Their lot was hard and bitter, even the merchants and better classes being oppressed and robbed mercilessly.

In 1521, when the nobles placed Estonia under the Swedish crown, the lot of the peasants was not improved, as in the transfer to Swedish sovereignty it was stipulated that the serfs should remain the property of their German owners, who sold them with the land as though they were cattle. After two hundred years of war, rebellion, and continued uprising Charles the third ceded Estonia to Russia in the Peace of Nystad, in 1721.

Peter the Great, who brought about the absorption of Estonia into the vast Russian Empire, had no interest in the personal troubles of the lower classes, and the Estonians had no hope of betterment until 1817, when Alexander I abolished serfdom by a royal ukase. This act brought great and temporary hope to the common people, but they soon learned that it was an idle gesture, given as a sop to world opinion and the demands of the Orthodox Eastern Church. The law was utterly ignored; the rich and powerful landowners continued to treat the peasants as chattels, and as a result bloodshed and revolt were the common order until 1881.

Then the Russians, tired with the interminable strife, made a strenuous effort to Russify the Estonians, and stern repressive measures were put into effect. The native language was forbidden, the ancient customs were proscribed, and new friction and fresh riots resulted in more bloodshed.

This was the situation up to 1914, when the World War began. The Russian arms did not prosper in that sad adventure, as you may recall, and both the army and navy of the Imperial force got a very rough deal, indeed! The army was especially neglected, the nobles and generals stealing most of the money that should have gone for munitions. When Russia had seventeen million men in uniform the entire army had only six million rifles, roughly one gun for every three soldiers. The great contractors were so afflicted with greed, that, with the connivance of grafting inspectors, they actually delivered ammunition filled with sand instead of gunpowder, and the army went into battle with supplies that were useless. While their man power was unlimited, their equipment was a farce. They never had more than 12% of the required number of machine guns for their infantry, and had only sixty batteries of field artillery where their organization called for three hundred and eighty-one! While they never won a major battle, *they lost between six and eight million men!* The exact number was never known, because the high command thought so little of the rank and file they did not keep accurate records of their losses.

The army and navy were on the edge of revolt when a strike occured on March 12, 1917, and the army was sent in to quell the striking workmen. Instead, the soldiers went over to the strikers and made common cause with them. Then the navy rebelled, and the Czar's government fell.

Kerensky took control until November seventh, and did his best to bring order out of chaos. His was an impossible task. He tried to carry on the war against Germany, settle the strikes, placate the army and navy, and organize a government that would really function. At this crucial hour the Bolsheviks struck, overthrew Kerensky, and seized the reins of power. They were welcomed into control primarily because of their major platform, which promised an immediate peace with Germany.

The Treaty of Brest-Litovsk was signed chiefly because the Russians were weary of war and sickened with constant defeat. The Germans played their cards well, and acted with traditional dis-regard for decency, honor, and fidelity to promises. In the first overtures the Germans assured the Russians that they would make no territorial demands and would ask for no monetary indemnity, and the peace conference began with that understanding. But as soon as the Russians laid down their arms, Germany acted with characteristic treachery and made stern demands as the price of peace. She took away from Russia the territories comprising Poland, Courland, Lithuania, Livonia, and Estonia, and forced Russia to pay an indemnity of three hundred million gold rubles!

The Ukrainians saw their opportunity in the squabble, and declared their independence of Russia, concluding a separate treaty of peace with Germany. After long and bitter debate and a renewal of hostilities Russia was forced to an ignominious surrender and signed the treaty which was forced on her at the point of the sword. The army refused to support the Bolshevik government, the people were so worn out with defeat they had lost all national pride, so Lenin and Trotsky signed the treaty because they were too weak to do otherwise. In this dark hour Russia lost 523,847 square miles of her territory! And temporarily, Estonia became a German possession.

Following the defeat of the Central Powers, the victorious allies had to decide the future of these embattled lands. Remember that Estonia had possessed no freedom or sovereignty for almost eight hundred years! She had been ruled by the Danes, the Swedes, the Teutonic Knights, the Germans, and had been under the Russian flag for exactly two hundred consecutive years.

On January 26, 1921, by an action of the Supreme Council of the Allied Powers, Estonia was declared a republic. On September 22 she was admitted as a member of the League of Nations, and on the 28th of the following January she was recognized by the United States as a sovereign state.

Quite naturally, the Russians never consented to this loss of territory, and planned to get it back. By means of communistic agitators they kept the little Republic stirred up and in a turmoil until the autumn of 1923, when the communistic party was outlawed by Estonia. On December first, a year later, three hundred communists attempted an armed coup with weapons supplied by the Russian government, but suffered a decisive defeat. The aroused Estonian officials stamped out all communistic elements ruthlessly, and a civil guard of 30,000 members was formed to preserve Estonian independence. Russia then quit, and made a non-aggression pact with Estonia, which was kept scrupulously by both sides. The two governments entered into peaceful and friendly relations until 1934.

At that time the Nazis began a campaign to occupy Estonia, and the communists quickly sprang into the battle. They renewed their activities and began to agitate for union with Russia. The Estonian government retaliated by abolishing all political parties and put the entire country under martial law. But when Hitler and Stalin made their famous non-aggression pact in 1939, Estonia became frightened of the Nazis and their probable designs on her, so they made a new pact with Russia. Under this agreement Estonia leased naval bases and airfields to Russia, and Russian troops were billeted in Estonia with her consent. The Estonians felt far safer with Russia than they did with Germany! When Russia began her war with Finland these bases were all used against the Finns, and proved of great value. In June of 1940, Russia became so alarmed by Germany's military successes she put in a huge army and occupied all of Estonia. In July of that same year a one-party "election" was held, and Estonia voted to become incorporated into the Soviet Union, and is today again back under the Russian flag.

The inspired architects of the coming perfect world, safely ensconced in Washington, have promised freedom, self-rule, and political sovereignty to *all* the nations of the earth. Only thus, the "Utopiacrats" state, can a lasting peace be assured. Now look at those promises in the light of the Estonian problem. If the Estonians decide to re-erect their shattered republic after this war and declare their independence of Russia, will the Bear lift his paw and let Estonia go? *He will not!* Then, are we committed by our promises to fight Russia for the freedom of Estonia? And if so, what has become of this promised peace?

Here are problems whose origins go so far back into past history that their antiquity approaches a thousand years. They have never been solved to the complete satisfaction of all parties concerned. Why do *we* think *we* are so much smarter than all the rest of mankind has been? Racial antipathies play as important a role as do the questions of geography, and are a pregnant course of trouble. To illustrate that fact, consider the issue of Livonia, which was at one time a province of Russia, but is now divided between Estonia and Latvia. The population was originally made up of the Livs, the Norova, the Chudes, the Semigallians, the Kors, and the Letgola. Since the ninth century they were all tributary to the Russian states, and the land has also had a stormy history. It has been ruled in turn by the Lithuanians, the Poles, the Swedes, and when Latvia and Estonia were formed into republics after World War One, the country was divided between them.

The surviving Letts are a proud and ambitious people, who have never been fully absorbed into neighboring races. They still have their own language and use the new form of common Lettish, which is displacing the numerous Lettish dialects which were once so common. They form an important fraction of several Baltic States, Estonia, Latvia, Lithuania in particular. In Latvia they constitute 77% of the population, and they insist upon their right to a domain and sovereign government that shall include all Letts in its sphere. They fought the Germans since the 13th century for the right of survival. Russia has never been able to absorb them, and their fierce desire for autonomy is a force to reckon with. To give them what they feel to be their ethnological and political due it would be necessary to disrupt the entire Baltic set-up, which would give rise to a dozen wars!

Not to weary the reader with a detailed resume of historical facts familiar to all, let us summarize it this way: after the disasterous defeat of 1917, and following the action of the Allies in 1918, Russia lost territories whose square area equalled the entire extent of our own states of California, Washington, Oregon, and Idaho! If the United States lost that much territory in war, what do you think our desire and ambition would be? Exactly: we'd never rest until we get it back, and Russia feels the same way! And she is going to regain that lost area if she has to fight the whole world to gain her rights.

Shall American blood be shed to prevent this?

Every true American will cry an instant, "NO!" and we should make our decision known on this matter in very strong terms. These are practical, historical facts, and they justify Russia in her claims and future plans. What can the idealists of Washington oppose to these known facts? They talk about permanent peace; in the face of these grave problems, how are they to achieve it? Neither ideals, ethics, charity, nor world opinion bear any weight with Stalin: force is the only God he recognizes. He frankly laughs at the high and noble phrases of the Atlantic Charter and expresses a frank disgust at the maukish vaporings of our alleged leaders! With commendable honesty Stalin has told the whole world what he plans to do, get, take, and hold: and what he has won by the sword he will not relinquish to orators! Can any sensible person see a basis for peace in these world conditions? We certainly do our cause no good by ignoring them.

Equally disturbing to future peace are Russia's aims in the Balkan States. Undoubtedly much of her future destiny lies in that direction, and her plans are certainly being laid with that idea in mind. It is only natural from every human viewpoint that Russia shall dominate the Balkan Peninsula. The first and main reason is ethnological. Since human conduct is the problem of the future, its incentives are to be found in ethnology even more than in geography. So while the Balkan States are divided into eight sovereign countries and governments (nine, if Turkey is included: although it is customary to count only European Turkey as part of the Balkan region), there are six major stocks in the populace, and five of them are fiercely nationalistic. The Albanians occupy part of the western mountain belt, and are largely Moslems. Their individuality is strongly developed and cherished. The Vlachs claim to be the descendants of the Roman conquerors and colonizers, later strengthened by refugees from the wars with the Barbarians. These Vlachs live a peculiar gypsy existence, subsisting by the practice of translocation. Their wealth consequently is in flocks and herds, and they practice no agriculture and have no interest in cities. They are highly assimilable, and mix with the Greeks and Servs so readily that they are gradually losing their social identity, but still remain a formidable people.

The Greeks are well known to the modern world, and even though they would have some difficulty proving their claim to descent from the classical Greeks of antiquity, they have inherited their traditions, their love of liberty, and many of their ideals. One of the strongest of these traits is the love of country and passion for political freedom, as the Greeks proved at terrific cost when they fought the combined might of the Axis Powers even though they foreknew the tragic end. They will never willingly yield the sovereignty of their land to any other power.

The Serbs and the Bulgars have been the most unhappy of the Balkan races, because of centuries of Turkish oppression. They are agricultural in their mode of living, and were easy victims of the Turkish conquests. Being tied to the soil, and not nomadic like the Vlachs, and dwelling in a country hard to defend, unlike the Albanians, the chains of virtual slavery were riveted upon them and maintained for generations.

The Bulgars suffered worst, being in the direct path of Turkish advance, and they possess an undying hatred for Turkey.

The most important racial group in the Balkans is the vast population of Slavs. Their immigration into the Balkan Peninsula began in the third century of the Christian era, and kept up for more than four centuries. By the end of the seventh century they had expelled or assimilated the original populace and were in virtual control of much of the region. By the tenth century they had built an empire which spread from the Adriatic to the Black Sea, ruling all the vast Balkan lands until overthrown by the Byzantine power in 1014 A. D.

These Slavs feel that their interests are bound to Russia by social ties, past history and future aspirations, and are quite cordial to any close alliance with Russia. The other peoples of the Balkans would rather trust Russia than Turkey, and if the close of this war finds Russia strategically prepared to expand into the Balkans, can the other powers stop her? Only by force of arms: and the perennial Balkan question holds plenty of promise of future trouble. These facts must be duly integrated into the plans for lasting peace, but the wide-eyed Pollyannas of political and ecclesiastical America blithely ignore them, and act as though they do not exist!

Another dark cloud rises on the horizon of world planning, and once again Russia is the unknown quantity. For centuries Russia has believed that her destiny demands control of the Dardanelles, the strait which connects the Black Sea with the Mediterranean. It has long been under the control of Turkey, and thus Russia is blocked from any egress from her own natural ocean lanes. It was the Russian attempt to wrest this control from Turkey which caused the Crimean war. The French, British, and Cardinians battled Russia from 1854 until 1856 to settle this issue, and the question is more alive today than it ever was before. It is a legitimate question to ask: "When Russia again presses her claims to the control of the Dardanelles, will the other great powers come to Turkey's aid and fight Russia once again?" And in that event, on which side will the United States be lined up? Who will get our lend-lease in that war, and on whose behalf will our blood then be spilled?

Yet one more sour note appears in the symphony of the coming peace, and that is Russia's position, place, and plans in the East. Her interests have settled in Persia for centuries, and now that the rejuvenated country is called Iran the interest remains as keen as it has always been. Russian activity in Persia began in the days of Peter the Great, who invaded Persia in 1722, and divided the country with the Turks, who also invaded Persia in 1724. After years of rebellion and warfare, during which the cost of occupation far exceeded the revenue derived, Russia voluntarily withdrew from Persia and restored her territory to the great warrior Nadir, who also expelled the Turks and the Afghans, and was consequently elected shah. Nadis has been recognized as the greatest of the Asiatic conquerors since Tamerlane, and was the last to deserve that title. He spent his life in battle and strife, and when he died, Persia was one of the most powerful of the nations.

British influence began in Persia in 1601, when trade was opened between the two powers, and the English helped the Persians win some important military victories. As the grip of Britain on India increased British and Persian interests became more closely knit, and when the Persians fought the Russians in 1812 and again in 1825 for the recovery of the lost province of Georgia, the English aided the Persians as far as they could without causing actual war between Britain and Russia. The defeat of Persia was disastrous, the shah signing a treaty which gave Russia permanent possession of Georgia and enabled her to claim three other provinces also. This caused fresh hostilities, but the Persians could not stand against the fierce and battle-loving Russians, and lost the sovereignty of their land to Russian commissioners. England and Russia then began a game that lasted a full century, with Persia as the political football in their activities!

In 1856 Great Britain declared war upon Persia because of the Afghan question, and Persia was quickly defeated and driven from Herat. She conceded the independence of Afghanistan, and the British made a most generous peace treaty, taking no indemnity nor territory. In the meantime Russia had advanced across Central Asia until she entirely enveloped the northern frontiers of Persia, and one at a time the border provinces were lost by annexation to Russia. After further bickering and sporadic warfare, in 1881 Russia finally compelled Persia to an abject acceptance of her loss of territory.

In the last few years of the 19th century, the Shah Muzaffar-ud-Din borrowed large sums of money from Russia, leaving Persia bankrupt and mortgaged to the Muscovite Government. Before his death in 1906 this shah was forced to establish a constitutional assembly, and the reform movement began. His successor attempted to crush the rising demand for popular government, but when he also came into armed conflict with Russia, was defeated and dethroned.

To revert back a few years, Russia and England almost went to war in 1885 over the question of control of Persia. Russia had designs on India, and would have pressed her ambitions there except for the disastrous war with Japan. The Russians expressed a desire for a friendly alliance with England who met them more than cordially. In the agreement each Power bound itself to respect the independence and sovereignty of Persia. They also designated the commercial spheres each Power was to occupy in future dealings with Persia, by which Russia was to have all rights in Northern and Central Persia, and Great Britain received commercial supremacy in the southern desert regions. History records that Britain dealt honestly, fairly, and benevolently with her section of Persia, but Russia was busy annexing the northern sections when the First World War halted her betrayal of the agreement. Since then the agreement has been annulled, and Persia is temporarily sovereign again.

The great query, which only time can solve, is the future attitude of Russia toward Persia, who she regards as a legitimate sphere of exploitation. Will Russia renew her march after the present war is ended? If so, she must possess Persia, and will England stand quietly by while Russia absorbs Persia? Or will she fight? And in that case, on whose side shall our sons die?

In any case, permanent peace rests upon a trembling and tottering foundation while such questions await future decision, which will probably be rendered by force of arms !

There is a significant suggestion which deserves mention here, made by the Prophet Ezekiel. In his description of the great battle of the Valley of Jehosaphat, which precedes the return of Christ in glory, Ezekiel lists the armed forces. He identifies Russia as the aggressor and leader of the invaders, and states that one of the accompanying allies is Persia. So it looks as though Russia is destined to dominate Persia, at the very least, and the fate of Persia is overshadowed by the Great Bear. The prophetic picture of Russia's future is dark, blood-drenched, and torn by strife. As long as the lusts and ambitions of this mighty power are not fulfilled, the strands of the fabric of the tapestry of peace are dyed with human blood. Peace is an idle dream in a future world where pride of race, greed for conquest, and the fierce love of liberty come into such sharp and continuous opposition.

One of the most evident facts of our day is the hypocracy of these political enchanters, who sing their promises of peace. Our government knows that they are idle, empty, and not capable of fulfillment. Every once in a while some high official of the inner circle makes a mistake, tells the truth, and lets the cat out of the bag! Such an instance occurred in the hearing of Congress over the proposed oil pipe line across the Arabian Desert. The International W. P. A.ers are all greatly interested in this project, which will cost the United States a vast sum, totaling multiplied scores of millions of dollars. Secretary of the Navy Knox testified before the committee that the pipe line was necessary for the successful prosecution of the war, as the fleet needed the oil. A committee member said that it would take *years* to put this pipe line in operation, and asked Secretary Knox how long he expected the war to last. Mr. Knox replied that he didn't mean the Navy would need the oil in *this* war: they wanted it ready for the *next* one!

What next one?

If we are about to embark upon an era of peace for generations, what war will we need this oil for? The stories do not hang together!

Of course, our rulers well know that the attainment of permanent peace by human efforts is a hopeless dream. Already the leaders in Washington are planning for the course of conduct we shall follow when peace comes. That includes the construction of a two-ocean navy that will be the mightiest fighting armada that ever floated.

We are planning for a standing army of two million men, and an active air force of a minimum of fifty thousand planes!

We are debating universal military training for all young men between the ages of 18 and 21, and to all of this I heartily agree. We want no future repetitions of Pearl Harbor! We never again want to put ourselves into such a helpless condition of unpreparedness that an aggressor will feel perfectly safe in assailing us. But while we are thus planning sensibly for future defense, why deceive ourselves with false promises of lasting peace?

Another disturbing factor is the lack of any concrete plan that will prevent the repetition of war. All our dreamy leaders, political or religious, chant in a unified chorus, "We must take steps to see that this never occurs again!" Ask them practically and plainly, "What steps do you plan or propose?" and you get a vacant stare as your only answer! The main trouble is that none of these Peace Planners have the courage to advocate any plan that would work! They want to coddle the defeated foe with such mawkish sentimentality that he will be *encouraged* to try again!

And yet it *is* possible to set up a peace plan that would bring a generation of rest from war. I do not say it will be done; in fact, I'm quite sure it won't. But let me set forth the conditions of such a plan as they occur to me. Call it "my peace plan" and let it go at that.

1) Make no peace treaty with Germany: just grant her a ten-year armistice, renewable for good behavior. During the time of this armistice, Germany to be occupied and governed by an allied council composed of hard-boiled military men, not by amateur politicians! (I do not say that this is right, or just, or brotherly; I just say that it would work! And since this is what Germany did to occupied France after her surrender, why should she not expect the same treatment?)

2) Permit no reconstruction to be done in Germany until the ravages of war in the invaded countries have all been repaired. The devastation committed by Germans in other lands, by German arms, should be repaired by a program of rebuilding by Germans at German expense.

3) Give Russia what she wants in the Baltic and Balkan States, as far as past history justifies her claims. (Again, I am not arguing the ethics or justice of this condition: I merely state *what would bring peace*. Russia is going to *take* what she wants if she can't get it any other way: why shed *our* blood to delay the inevitable?)

4) Give half of Prussia to restored Poland, to compensate her for the territory she will be compelled to surrender to Russia. (When Germany objects to this condition, remind her that this is what she planned to do to Poland and other countries; we got the idea from her!)

5) Divide the rest of Germany into separate states, provinces, or duchies, refusing them the right to maintain stand-

ing armies, to manufacture or acquire weapons of war, or to build or have a navy.

6) Compel all veterans of the German army which destroyed Europe, to rebuild Europe by forced labor, compensating them by food, shelter and clothing only. In other words, apply to them the same harsh conditions they forced upon the people of the occupied countries.

(If they learned that a defeated army had to stay and "clean up" after itself, they might hesitate before starting another mess. Why should they who caused havoc twice in one generation escape all punishment and payment?)

7) Dismember the Japanese Empire, stripping her of all territory except her original home islands. That means the return of Korea to the Koreans, or Formosa and Manchukuo to China.

8) Seize all Japanese treasure, gold, art, and other valuable property that can be applied to the repayment of the damage she has caused China, the Philippines, and the Dutch and other territory she has invaded.

In a word, make the losers *pay* and they will be less likely to gamble again! The practical side of this brutal plan is in the guarantee it would offer for the safeguarding of peace, because of the fact that the traditional aggressors would thus be rendered and kept too weak to assail their neighbors. I realize, of course, that certain factors will prevent any such plan as here suggested from being put into practice. One of the chief of these is the suspicion with which the Great Powers view each other, and the ambitions they all have for increasing their domains and their spheres of influence. Great Britain fears the expansion of Russia, and rightly so. They have been rivals for a century or more, in which time the British have been on top with commendable consistence. But it begins to look as though Russia may emerge from the present war in a dominant position, and will be faced with the opportunity of making herself the chief world power in ten years. So Great Britain would like to have some other European state or states strong enough to act as a check upon Russia, but weak enough to be no great danger to Britain. Hence her statesmen will strive to retain for Germany a united and sovereign dominion, weakened just enough to discourage aggression. In which case Germany will try it again. She has been the aggressor in *two hundred and twelve* wars of conquest in two thousand years, the two greatest of which were fought in our own times.

For reasons of policy, Russia also desires a German state that can be used as a check on the expansion of Great Britain. Russia will inevitably find herself in collision with British interests in the Balkans, the Near East, and the Far East as well. Only France desires the complete subjugation of Germany, and her voice will count for little or nothing when the terms of peace are finally laid down.

The leaders of the United States are the least reliable of all in the present world! They are influenced by the triple motives of sentimentality, politics, and expediency. Our present rulers not only desire to perpetuate themselves and their anti-American bureaucracy in power, but they dream of extending their social experiments to the rest of the planet. Hence our so-called foreign policy is a joke among the councils of the nations and partakes of the ability of the chameleon to change its color instantly, so as to blend with its temporary surroundings. If the present party remains in power until the armistice, our voices will only add to the confusion that will ensue. The most vociferous ideologists who can influence the most votes will be heeded first, and the practical gains that might have been won will all be dissipated before the agreement is ratified. Beyond question Stalin will all but dictate the terms to which the rest of the United Nations will have to agree. Out of the coming peace conference will emerge the blueprint for the next war, and we may as well open our eyes to that distressing prospect.

Does the organized Church of Christ *want* to take the responsibility for setting up the conditions of peace under these circumstances? If the destiny of the Church is linked to the prospects of maintaining world peace, the Church is doomed! She will be well advised to keep her consecrated nose out of other people's business! Only an apostate church is concerned with an attempt to bring peace by covenant; the true and believing church knows that world politics are not her mission. She was erected by God to *evangelize,* not to interfere in the perishing world systems which are doomed by the prophetic Word. If the Church would purge her ranks of infidelity and modernism in its every guise, and go back to her ancient dictum, "Ye must be born again" she could do far more to promote world peace than she can ever accomplish by butting into inter-national conferences. We have no right to representation at the peace conference as a Church, any more than the Democrats, the Republicans, the Socialists, and the Communists have as party organizations. Indeed, we have far less right there as an organization, since their chief interest is in politics and human government, and our sole purpose is the salvation of men. Since wars all come from lust, (James 4:1,2) we cannot hope to have peace in an unconverted world. Certainly the modern "social gospel," which concerns itself exclusively with the present world and the body of man, can offer no solution to the problem of war and its eradication. No matter how clean the environment of a sinner may be, or how perfect his conditions of living, he still has an evil heart and the lust for power ,wealth, conquest, and self-glory. The only way to change human relations is to transform humans: and that can only be accomplished by the regeneration of the individual. When a majority of earth's population is composed of Christians who know they have been born again, and are walking in the way of God's will, there will be no wars. So our hope for the future and our greatest contribution to human welfare is in evangelization. Let us carry the Cross of Christ to this perishing world, knowing no message but Jesus Christ, crucified, and we can serve our own generation effectively and bring hope to those who follow after us.

This present mad campaign of Protestant leaders for a hand in the designing of the peace plan springs from ignorance of the Word of God, or more probably from unbelief in that Word. The promises and warnings of prophecy are historically reliable. They have never failed in the past, hence they are accredited for the future. And all the teachings of prophecy coincide in the conclusion that there can be no lasting peace until Jesus Christ comes again. Indeed, how can a race that is in rebellion against God hope for, or expect peace? "There *is* no peace" saith my God—"To the Wicked!" So the warnings of the entire prophetic section of the Holy Bible all state in terms of finality that wars will recur and endure while Jesus is absent from this earth. This plain statement of Holy Writ is rejected by the Council of Bishops, who simply do not believe the Bible. Indeed, they profess to know more than Jesus Christ on this issue! Although they take His name and call themselves His disciples, they deny His authority and calmly repudiate Him as creditable teacher and leader.

For Jesus stated in terms a child could not misunderstand, that wars would continue for the entire duration of the Gospel age. He prophecied that nations and kingdoms would rise in armed conflict against each other until the very hour of His return—but our Bishops and liberal leaders of "another gospel" scoff at the words of Christ, and seek to regiment us into a concerted drive to effect peace by covenant, in spite of the historical evidence that such will not work, and in defiance of the warnings of Our Lord Jesus Christ!

If the Church follows these vicious counsels the church is doomed. This is a very present crisis, and one we have to face. If we hitch our wagon to the star of permanent peace, and the star fades out or explodes, our motive power is gone and so is our influence and authority. Indeed, I have heard many hundreds of men in our armed forces sneer at Christianity and ridicule the Church for just this reason. They maintain (and not without considerable justice) that the preachers have spent twenty years declaring there could be no more war: that war was wicked, sinful, and never justified, and flooded America with the propaganda of pacifism; then, these men complain, as soon as war started these preachers all changed their tune. They rushed into uniform as chaplains, got a commission, and a better salary than they ever had before, went out with a Bible in one hand and a flag in the other, in neither one of which they had previously believed to any great extent!

That is a brutal indictment of modernism and pacifism, the Siamese-twin evils that brought the organized church to the confessedly low ebb of 1939. Shall we repeat this grave error and worship the false gods and vain philosophies of worldly leaders in eccliastical robes, or shall we forsake the altars of scholarly idolatry and turn back to the clear teachings of the Word of God? The Church must make the choice, and upon the wisdom of that choice depends her survival as a great organization. Our hope of future greatness and our opportunities for service to mankind are irrevocably united to the Gospel of redemption by faith in Jesus Christ. Through the faithful proclamation of this message only can we survive and prosper in a warring world.

Chapter IV

THE CHURCH OF CHRIST, AND THE NEW WORLD ORDER

ONCE again our ears are ringing with the clarion voices of wild enthusiasts, who promise us a perfect world as soon as the war ends, and whose chants differ no whit from the same empty promises that deluded the gullible in past decades. The most impossible ideals are advocated with no sensible program of implementation, and a perfect world is definitely promised by each school of social culture, if we will but turn the government of this world over to them and let them put their theories into practice. The fact that these schemes and systems have brought chaos to our own internal affairs and transformed us from a solvent democracy into a bankrupt bureaucracy does not dim the ardor of these self-appointed leaders: they are quite confident that their plans will function, even though the details thereof are contrary to every known law of human behavior.

This is no new experience for the race: every recent generation has felt its own sad failure and has dreamed of a brighter future for those who follow. After generations of repeated mistakes we *should* show some improvement in human relations, but the present age is characterized by the identical philosophy of conquest that actuated Chaldea and Babylon in their day.

There is no difference between the treatment of enslaved Israel in Egypt in the days of Pharoah, and murdered Israel in Germany today—except that Pharoah dealt a little more

kindly with his slaves than Hitler has done, and Egypt, priz-
ing the labor of Israel, did not torture its Jews in concentra-
tion camps.

The picture is further darkened by the actuating philosophy
which causes one nation to exalt itself as a super-race, divinely destined to rule the earth, and hence legitimately entitled
to slaughter lesser people on the sole excuse that they are
slave, or non-Aryan. The Roman riveted no more onerous
chains upon the countries they conquered than the Nazis
do today, and as long as nations that hold to the basic principles which operate in Japan and Germany still exist on this
planet, there can be no hope of a perfect civilization.

But this present dream of a "new world order" especially
expresses the psychology of two great groups. The first is the
mass of any generation which is wearied by a great war. There
is no new note in the present chorus of wishful thinkers—at
least not for those of us who remember the dark days of 1914
to 1918. Then, as now, we were worn with the struggle and
sick of sacrifice and bloodshed, and were easily persuaded that
the war we then fought would be the last one in history, and
that out of the settlement would rise the golden age when men
would study strife no more. Certainly no more noble set of
inter-national principles and procedures was ever concocted
than the famous "Fourteen Points" enunciated by Woodrow
Wilson, and if any plan of peace preservation would work,
that one should have succeeded. But the notable President left
out of his calculations one vital factor; the sinful nature of
man! The ill-starred League of Nations became the most
colossal failure of history; the very divisions of territory which
were made to guarantee the rights of smaller nations resulted
in war after war; and the present conflict developed out of
the failure of the rosy but impractical plans that were made
and erected upon the false foundation of the brotherhood of
man.

We seem doomed to repeat that same tragic train of errors again. Shutting our eyes to the lessons of history, the basic principles of economics, and the clear warnings of the Word of God. We are attempting also to erect a permanent peace upon a foundation of theory; and we, too, dream of a new order in which peace, righteousness, good will, and security will prevail. This is a common war-time psychological phenomena.

The other group, which naturally turns to ideas of a new world order as an escape from reality, is composed of those who have suffered great loss through war, and dream of recovering their honor and possessions in some spectacular fashion. This is the one certain explanation of Hitler's phenominal rise to power. He came to a Germany smarting under the sting of defeat, and made bitter by the loss of a vast colonial empire; promising them complete recovery of all they had forfeited, won the German people to blind allegiance and acceptance of his principles and plans. Because he was the one man who had a comprehensive program, he became the logical candidate for the post of savior, and all the disgruntled of the nation fell into step with his suggestions. Very eminent German business men told me quite frankly on a visit to Germany, that while they did not approve of some of the Fuehrer's acts, he had their complete confidence and backing because he had the one sure means of regaining all that the nation had lost through the bitter defeat of 1918. So the Germans began to dream of a "new world order" in which they would be the master race; in which all lesser peoples would exist as slaves, laboring for the comfort and enrichment of their German masters, and in which the former victors over German arms would lie crushed and humiliated by German military genius.

Benito Mussolini rose to power upon this identical principle, and was swept along to heights of greatness by this same impulse. Italy paid a bitter price for her participation in World

War One; although she never won a major victory, she lost over five hundred thousand men who were casualties! She had been promised certain rewards for her efforts on the allied side, but when the great division was made Italy got nothing. Indeed, when Turkey, one of the defeated enemies drew sword against Italy and seized certain islands the Italians possessed, the League of Nations sat quietly and let her member be robbed. To assuage the wounded feelings of his nation and to possess himself of some of the spoils, Mussolini invaded friendly and peaceful Ethiopia, and the Italian forces indulged in such brutality and murder as recent history cannot excell. In so doing, Mussolini boasted that he had revived and re-erected the Roman Empire; Italy's king assumed the title of Emperor, and a new world order was proclaimed for the Italian people.

Hence we should recognize in practical historical realism the fact that our present propaganda for a "new world order" is not novel or unique—it is the natural expression of a generation that is tired of repeated strife.

Of course, *our* plan is different! We do not plan an era of dominance and empire, but rather hope to bring in a Golden Age in which every day will be Christmas, and Uncle Sam will be the perpetual Santa Claus. One of our greatest Utopiacrats has expressed our platform for the post-war world in five separate but related planks, as: "To bring to all races: 1) enduring peace, 2) prosperity, 3) culture, 4) political freedom, and 5) economic stability."

This is a large order! Since we cannot even guarantee these five blessings to our own national population, how are we going to make them effectively available to the whole world? In fact, the allied leaders all know that this is an utter impossibility. Nations *do not* learn by trial and error: they merely repeat their errors in each generation, and bring upon themselves the same old trials! Here is a quotation from Winston

Churchill which sounds as though he spoke it yesterday, as he faced the hope of a coming peace. Note and heed his words:

> "It is a tale that is told, from which we may draw the knowledge and comprehension needed for the future. The disproportion between quarrels of nations and the suffering which fighting out those quarrels involves; the poor and barren prizes which reward sublime endeavor on the battle field; the fleeting triumphs of war; the long, slow rebuilding; the awful risks so hardily run; the doom missed by a hair's breadth, by the spin of a coin, by the accident—all this should make the prevention of another great war the preoccupation of mankind."

Does that paragraph have a fimiliar sound? Of course it does, it might have been broadcast over the B. B. C. yesterday. But it was written and uttered in 1929—and then years later the world was in flames again! It takes far more than the knowledge of what is good and what is evil to keep mankind walking in the paths of rectitude, and the fact that war "does not pay" has never brought peace to any generation. And no wide-awake, practical, sensible thinker has any faint hope or remote belief, that an era of peace and common prosperity lies ahead of our age. The advocates of the mythical new order, of which we hear so much today, are largely deluded theologians who live with their heads in bright clouds of impractical theories; college professors who would starve to death in a factual world outside of the class-room; or political schemers who desire the resources of the United States Treasury to finance their grandiose socialistic projects on a world-wide scale.

It is a strong statement to make, but it is self-evident that alert world-leaders know that the present high-sounding ideals and proposed projects are impossible of attainment. This is manifest when we consider their actions and contrast their conduct with their conversations! Their words that are uttered for publicity do not coincide with the plans they are making for the future. As an instance, we have already referred to the fact that our own Government is planning for a huge army and a colossal two-ocean navy when this present war ends—for what? If we are to have enduring peace and a world order in which contentment is the rule, we shall need no army, and a navy would be useless! But we are ruled, fortunately, by men of common sense, and these men know that the armistice will *not* result in the regeneration of the race, and that the defeated peoples will probably try again. Hence they wisely plan to have us prepared. They also realize that some nations who are allies now may be our opponents in a decade or two, and all sensible citizens heartily approve of and commend plans for future national defense! Why, then, do we talk one way, and think and act another?

Our administration, in the midst of the worst war history has ever recorded, is even now making commitments and drawing up treaties of mutual aid and military help in the case of future need. This is highly commendable, and our security in the years ahead may well depend upon such wise arrangements being made now. But why should we be concerned about out-lying bases, island strongholds, far-flung lines of defense, and huge reserve arsenals if it is true that we are about to erect a new world order in which stability and security will be assured all men? I repeat the assertion: our leaders know that these fantastic promises are not capable of being fulfilled, and the new order as described and propagated is impossible. Why should the Church of Christ lay aside her distinctive message and surrender her unique mission to assume leadership in political schemes that cannot be made to function? As Isaiah cried out to Israel centuries ago: "Our strength is to sit still!"

The wild vaporings of the paid orators who eulogize the new order cannot be translated into reality, for many reasons.

Look at the world in which we live as it actually is, and not as it appears through the rose-colored spectacles of social dreamers, and you will realize that fact. There are hundreds of millions of the earth's population living under conditions which make their prosperity, for instance, impossible. The second plank in the idealist's platform is universal prosperity: how can we bring that to pass?

As a concrete illustration, consider the fellahin of Egypt. The word "fellah" denotes the peasant class, the plural form being "fellahin." They constitute one of the most poverty-stricken groups of human beings on the face of our planet. This condition is inevitable in the light of the social, religious, and economic systems under which they live, and is due also to the form of government that prevails in that ancient land. The fellahin are the laborers and tillers of the soil, and since agriculture is the chief industry and almost the only source of wealth in Egypt, the fellahin constitute the greater proportion of the population. Over sixty-two percent of the population of this grim land engage in agriculture: about ten percent of the total population are tradesmen, or practicing some profession of skilled trade. Since fourteen-fifteenths of the area of Egypt is desert, the fifteen million inhabitants are necessarily crowded on the cultivable lands and in the cities, which though few in number, hold twenty percent of the population. Few countries have ever suffered greater loss of human life due to mis-government, yet the people have a vitality which enables them to regain their losses whenever conditions are relieved. At the beginning of the British occupation in 1882, the population of Egypt was a little over six million: when the British retired in 1937, the people numbered between fifteen and sixteen million! They seem utterly incapable of intelligent self-government, and are consistently robbed and plundered from generation to generation. Their happiest days have always been under benevolent foreign rule.

Let us examine the lot of these fellahin, in the light of their living conditions. They are bound to the land, and are little better than draft animals. The state is the ultimate proprietor of all lands, and grants a life-tenancy to a favored landlord class, who thus have the enjoyment of three-fourths of the cultivable land. Acreage held under this title is known as "Kharaji lands" and are distinct from the "Ushuri lands" which are held in fee-simple, subject to an annual rent paid to the government in the form of exorbitant taxes. The basic measure is the "Feddan" which is equivalent to $333\frac{1}{3}$ square kassabah, which is so close to a yard that we can say a feddan is about one and four-hundredths acres in extent.

One million, six thousand landlords own less than five feddans! They do not work this land, but lease it to fellahin on share-crop terms, so that a fellah must earn his living, pay his taxes and raise his family on one half the income from less than five acres! Many of them have as little as an acre or even one-half an acre to cultivate, and they are a lean and hungry group even in good times. Ninety percent of the fellahin never know what it means to go to bed at night having had enough food to satisfy their hunger for that one particular day.

Their financial status can best be understood by the coinage of the country. The monetary basis is the pound Egyptian, which is valued at about six-pence more than the British pound. The Egyptian pound is divided into 100 piastres and 1,000 milliemes; the millieme being in turn divided into coins called paras, one para being one-fortieth of a millieme. To compare it to our coinage we can say a piastre equals a nickel, hence a millieme would be a half a cent. Therefore there would be eighty paras to one American penny, and when people are so poor they deal in coins that have a value of one-four-hundredth of a nickel, they are poor indeed! Sixty percent of Egypt's population earn their living under conditions such as these, and our wild-eyed American administrators are promising them, among other things, prosperity!

Contrast their lot to the fortunate owners of large lands, who number twelve thousand persons holding title to over fifty feddans of rich soil. This fortunate class coin the sweat and hunger of the fellahin into gold for their own coffers, and live in luxury and splendor. Egypt could produce wealth and plenty for its entire population if honor, fairness, and generosity were not absolute strangers to the Egyptian culture and system of government. The king of Egypt is one of the wealthiest humans alive. He has a personal fortune of some fifty millions of dollars, and receives a "salary" from the state of four hundred thousand dollars a year, and in addition has all of his living expenses paid out of the taxes raised from the people. He lives in the most dazzling splendous enjoyed by any monarch in history, and the food that is daily served in his palace, where solid gold service is provided for six hundred guests, would feed the poor of vast Cairo.

To change the condition of the fellahin it would first be necessary to completely revise the Egyptian system of economics. But this in turn is based upon their form of government, which in turn derives from the Mohammedan religion. And since fourteen out of fifteen Egyptians are Moslems, to change their religion is an almost impossible task. The heartless creed of Islam sees no wrong in the poor being enslaved by the rich, it must be the "will of Allah" or it would not so be! Remembering that the Egyptians are fiercely determined to preserve their recently secured political freedom from foreign powers, and considering the fanaticism with which they cling to the tenets of Mohammed: and in the light of the fact that self-government and freedom of political systems is also a basic guarantee of the promised new order, how do we propose to bring prosperity, economic stability, and political emancipation to this nation of serfs?

Does the Church want to take this impossible task on her self—or shall she revert to the old method of evangelizing such a land, confident that a people set free by the Gospel of Jesus Christ will in time solve their own basic problems?

What does the new world order plan to do with India, the world's gravest present problem? Are these five guarantees intended to apply to that country and to those people; and if so, how do we propose to assure India "enduring peace, prosperity, culture, political freedom, and economic stability"? The population of India numbers 339 million: which is one-fifth of the entire human family. This is about the equal of the population and area of all Europe, with the exception of Russia, and the natives of India are no more united and homogeneous than are the peoples of Europe. The Indians are divided into eight distinct racial types, widely diverse in their interest, history, religion and culture, and possessing a long tradition of warfare with each other.

When you consider an attempt to mould them into one political pattern, remember that these 339 million people speak 222 different languages, dialects and vernaculars, and that many millions of them cannot understand or converse with many other millions of their fellow countrymen. How shall we weld such a mass of divided humans into one united nation?

Consider the diversity of their religions, which question generally proves to be the most difficult to solve, and in the fanaticism of which we are apt to find the most diversive factors. Catalogue them briefly as follows:

Hindus—239 Million: divided into 7 sects.

Mohammedans—78 million: divided into 10 sects.

Buddhist—13 million: divided into 9 sects.

Sikhs—4½ million: constituting a sect of Moslems, but counted apart from them.

Jains—1¼ million:

Christians—6½ million: divided into all known denominations.

Animists—8¼ million:

Parsees—110 thousand.

Does any intelligent person honestly believe that, in the present state of humanity and in the face of conflicting interests, ambitions, and allegiances, it is possible to quickly get this weird mess together into a functioning and efficient form of self-rule? For centuries the Mohammedans and the Hindus have been at swords points, and neither sect will yield the chief authority to the other. Their very basic beliefs are incompatible and irreconcilable, and if the strong hand of Great Britain were removed, or her wise counsel withdrawn, the wretched land would be bathed in the blood of civil war for decades to come. The dreamers of political autonomy for all peoples will find a rude awakening when they attempt to establish this Utopian ideal in India!

As for a common culture, the very hope of raising India to our own educational level is doomed by the fact that only seven per cent of the population is literate to the extent that they can read and write a simple sentence in their own tongue. To educate the mass of India we would have to translate our text book into 222 vernaculars, or teach 339 million people to read English! Since 93 per cent of the population of India is utterly illiterate, they are natural victims of propaganda in its most vicious forms, being lead by rabble rousers and lurid orators, who tell them the most incredible tales and are assured of belief because of the ignorance of the listeners. Fertile grounds for discontent and strife are thus always available to those who would provoke trouble to advance their own personal and selfiish interests, and cohesion for self betterment cannot be achieved by India.

The "economic stability" promised by our International New Dealers is one of the most improbable of all their hopes and dreams. Remember that seventy-five per cent of India's masses earn their living directly through agriculture. The crops depend in large measure upon the strange phenomenon of seasonal rains, called the monsoons, which saturate the soil for weeks and make it possible for the land to produce. When the monsoon fails to arrive, as it occasionally does, that dread tragedy the world has often seen, an "Indian Famine" results, and multitudes die of hunger. The British government cannot be praised too highly for the manner in which it has planned and striven to develop irrigation systems in much of India's best farming regions, often against the will and over the bitter opposition of the natives who were to benefit thereby. The persistence of the British has now made it possible to irrigate about one fifth of the farms, and famines in that area are now no longer a danger.

Even though the British occupation of India has raised the per capita income of the natives some three hundred per cent, it is still true that ninety per cent of the people earn less than a bare subsistence. The balance must be supplied by charity or government doles, or by tax-supported projects. In our bright new world, what practical method shall be used to deal with this particular condition, and how long will it be before the plan begins to work?

One of our best minds at Washington recently expressed the ideas and ideals of the New World architects in these words:

> "The United Nations are fighting to make a world in which tyranny and aggression cannot exist: a world based upon freedom, equality, and justice: a world in which all persons regardless of race, color or creed may live in peace, honor and dignity."

If that were indeed the purpose for which we now wage war, this would be a holy war indeed! But is it? Is Russia, for instance, fighting to bring about the conditions set forth in that beautiful and poetic passage of fiction? I rather gathered that Russia was fighting to preserve for herself, her own territory, and political system. That Russia *became* a "United Nation" in the sense of this citation only when her former partner, Germany, attacked her and invaded her land is a fact of history! Great Britain is certainly not fighting to bring about the Utopian condition described by this Brain Trust enthusiast: Winston Churchill says that *they* are in battle to preserve their empire and their very right to live. The United States is in this war because Japan bombed Pearl Harbor and treacherously invaded the Philippines, and we are fighting for the same basic reason a cornered animal launches an attack!

But now that necessity has drawn us into this grim and sombre struggle, can we coin it into a virtue and accomplish the purpose of this statement? The Utopiacrat said "the world"— he included "all persons, regardless of race, creed or color." That certainly includes India, a few factors of whose problem we have just listed. We are entitled to ask the designers of this new World of Tomorrow "How do you plan to achieve the political freedom and guarantee the economic stability of a heterogeneous mass such as the population of India?" Incidently, these same great-hearted saviors of all the world are the identical folks who failed to guarantee or secure our *own* stability and economic security! How are they going to do for the *world* what they could not accomplish in their own nation?

The noble and high-sounding phrases of the famed "Atlantic Charter" will not do it, no matter how sincere the promises and premises of that document were, no practical method has been suggested for implementing those promises. And even as I write, new conferences are being held to modify this "charter," and to decide to whom it applies, and to what extent its promises can be guaranteed to which nations!

Politicians cannot bring about this Golden Age: the dreamers of the District of Columbia can't even decide in which direction Utopia lies; how then can they show us the way? In fact, every little group of self-appointed political messiahs advocates a different route to nowhere, and if we tried to sort out their solo voices from the din of the chorus, we would all soon be as daft as they appear to be!

Can science remake the world, and bring in this Golden Age? *Not unless it discovers how to change human nature!* I do not attempt to minimize the benefits that have come to man through scientific research, for by such aid we are well on the way to a conquest of the physical earth with all of its treasures and resources. Such a conquest will truly give us possession of the vast heritage the Creator intended us to possess some day, but in that very fact lies our gravest danger. Man's control over his own nature has not kept pace with his increasing control over the forces of nature! Envy, cruelty, hatred, greed, selfishness, malice, falsehood, and mass murder are the chief notes in the funeral march to which civilization is keeping step today, and man is the present victim of his own scientific advancement. Another generation of research and improved weapons will give mankind the tools to destroy a major portion of the human race, and unless he can master *himself*, the race is doomed. And this is the one thing that science *cannot* help him to accomplish.

Indeed, science is not looking unto man for the solution of his major problems, but is rather looking *out* from man to the complete conquest of his environment. In an address before the Baconian Club of the University of Iowa, October 8, 1943, Dr. George Glockler said:

"Will the human race have to go through an abyss of darkness, which is war, at periodic intervals; or is there hope that a new and more abundant civilization can appear on the surface of this earth? Scientifically trained men believe that the economic basis of human existence on the planet will be so profoundly affected by future scientific learning, discovery, and invention, and the subsequent repercussions in the economic sphere will be of such magnitude that an age of plenty will be initiated where the present economic and political struggles between empires will tend to disappear. Perhaps no individual can offer at the moment a reasonable solution of current international difficulties as long as millions of people need food and clothing of which there is a scarcity. War and strife may be inevitable in a world in which fifty percent of the wealth is enjoyed by about six percent of the population. It is to be hoped that future generations will solve the problems of distribution of wealth on a more equable basis so that they may look back upon the present period with horror and unbelief, wondering how the social and economic injustice of today could ever have been perpetrated by so-called human beings."

This eminent scientist and educator went on to develop in a fascinating and capable manner his main thesis; that a better civilization will be made possible because science will revolutionize the economic system of the earth, and there will be plenty for all. Note that all of the improvement is in environment, not in individuals: the program is to be made in physical substances, not in the will, morals, or soul of man.

There seems to be a contradiction here. The administrators of the United States claimed that they would bring economic stability to the country by *limiting* production, the scientists hope to bring prosperity and freedom to the world by *increasing* production! They can't both be right, and it is highly probable that they could both be wrong! For instance, I have noticed that the very wealthy of the present world system are not at peace with themselves or each other, although they are free from the shadow of want, and exempt from the strife of competition. They have a record of divorce that exceeds any other group, they are in trouble with the law and in many cases seem to be utterly unmoral in their basic conduct. I am not forgetting the other side of the picture, and recognize that many men and families of great wealth have written a great record of godliness and benevolence that deserves the highest commendation. I merely cite the other group to refute the theory that tolerance, stability, peace, and universal prosperity depend largely or entirely upon physical assets! Science can arm us with mighty forces: it cannot control or direct our use or misuse of those vast powers. Anger or inordinate ambition may lead men to divert these new powers to destructive ends, and science knows no control for human emotions and motives.

At the climax of a recent motion picture "Madame Curie," the leading character delivered, a long and beautiful homily eulogizing science and extolling its gifts to man. She climaxed her oration by depicting a perfect world of peace and plenty all made certain in the future by the benefits and blessing of science. Not one word of God, or the redeeming grace of Jesus Christ was ever introduced into the modus operandi by which this dream was to be realized; which is not surprising when we remember that Madame Curie was an absolute and confirmed atheist. The plans of the godless should hold no allure for the Church of Christ, and we have seen the results of human planning too often to place much faith in the new ideas of a perfect world, brought about by methods that have failed repeatedly in past generations!

There is no substitute for regeneration!

The only thing wrong with humanity is human nature. Change that for the better, and the world is improved to the extent of mankind's victory over his own nature. A new world order cannot be built upon a foundation of selfishness and greed—sinners cannot erect a sinless state!

There *is* a formula that would effect a perfect national and international comity, but it would have to be universally applied without exception. That technique is written in the words of Jesus in John 3:7, "Marvel not that I say unto you, ye must be born again!" There is no problem of human conduct or relations that cannot be solved by this formula, and no new world order will emerge in any lasting form if erected upon any other premise.

Have you ever catalogued the immediate and imperative problems that have to be solved in a comprehensive and satisfactory manner, before the glittering promises now made so glibly can be translated into reality? Take time to list a few, then search for a permanent and quick solution for each of them. Consider these:

Item: Out of the present conflict there will emerge a Russia armed to the teeth, flushed with victory, justly proud of military accomplishments that have no parallel in the past century. Her interests are purely and passionately Russian, and she has stated her intention of repossessing herself of all the ancient lands that once were gathered under the Russian flag, and of dominating all neighboring territories that can affect her future security, her manifest destiny, or her natural expansion. She has no illusions of securing stability and political freedom for every race under the sun, and has no inhibitions against force or arms as a means of attaining her goals. How do our present exponents of a new order plan to integrate Russia into their blue print for this grand and laudable scheme?

Item: When Germany is beaten to her knees, there will be a vast army of ten million young fanatics, schooled in the psychology and ideals of Nazi philosophy, who will form the nucleus of Germany's next army and the main spring of her next attempt at world conquest. They will be writhing in the bitterness of military defeat, and will live for the single purpose of revenge. They cannot be "re-educated" into a better frame of mind—their mental processes are fixed and closed to any outside illumination. From the cradle they have been tutored and hardened in the psychology of conquest, and they are the permanent fruits of Hitler's system of schooling. They sincerely believe they are destined to be the masters of the earth, and defeat will be received by them as a mere temporary set-back, delaying their triumph, but not obviating it by any means. They will be as a cancer in the body of world politics, and short of shooting all ten million of them, how do we propose to keep them from upsetting the program of universal stability and economic, political, and religious freedom for all races and creeds?

Item: The Oriental philosophy which makes the "loss of face" intolerable, will drive Japan into fevered endeavors to prepare for a second attempt at conquest, and as long as they are allowed autonomy they will sacrifice and suffer to make themselves ready for their next great adventure. "Our plan" calls for absolute freedom, remember, for *all* races: hence if we deny Japan the opportunity for self-rule, for stability, and prosperity which our scheme calls for, we defeat our purpose in this glad "new era." So what do we plan to do with the defeated countries, and how do they fit into our five-fold guarantee to all men?

Item: Winston Churchill has repeatedly asserted that the British Empire does not intend to relinquish a square yard of its vast territory, and that Great Britain is not fighting at such sacrifice and cost merely to see the dissolution of her empire. How, then, can we bring our five universal blessings to the subject peoples and native tribes of the British Empire, and how can we have this new world order if we leave them out of the benefits?

Item: When the present war ends, China faces the danger of a vast civil war. This threat is so real that it amounts almost to a certainty. Mighty factions are arrayed against each other in that troubled land, and forces that are diametrically opposed to each other tear their unity into shreds. We guarantee all peoples political freedom: how is the question of their own form of government to be settled in China? Russia is even now stirring up the troubled issue of Communism, and the arms we now export to China for the defeat of Japan will probably be used by Chinese armies representing different ideologies against each other. Can our bright minds at Washington solve this issue?

Remember that we have promised all races and colors "economic stability" as well as political freedom. China has a population of almost unbelievable magnitude, the exact number being difficult to estimate. An accurate and scientific census is not possible, and the best and most recent careful estimate sets the figure at considerably over 485 million. To this must be added the 11 million additional inhabitants of Mongolia, Tibet, and Sinkiang. We have nearly a half billion humans to deal with in all China! This vast population dwells in an area of 4,277,260 square miles, which huge territory is divided geologically, and separated politically into at least eight definite regions. The interests of the different groups of Chinese are as wide and conflicting as are the interests of Africa and Mexico, or any other two races who differ radically.

About 80 per cent of China's population depend upon agriculture for their livelihood, and the average income and level of subsistance are appallingly low. In certain districts the population averages over 2,000 per square mile, and in these centers over 50 per cent of the people have incomes well below the poverty line. So we have here a country which is in reality a continent, peopled by a half billion human beings, who, while diverse in interests, and political, religious, and occupational aspirations, are nevertheless closely knit by a culture that pervades the entire race and that has been practically unchanged for four thousand years.

We now propose and promise to bring to them "enduring peace, prosperity, culture, political freedom and economic stability"—and we further guarantee to them an existence "based upon freedom, equality and justice . . . wherein they may live in peace, honor and dignity."

Will some one of these land promisers kindly tell us just how they intend to bring all of this to pass? In this new world order, erected by the dreamers on paper, what method will be used to solve the problems of China?

Item: How do our rulers plan to solve the perplexing problem of our own minority groups right here in the United States of America? There is a vast amount of agitation among American Pink Leaders, publicists and fellow-travelers of the Communistic party-line over the immediate freeing of poor, enslaved India. How about the American Negro, for instance? Where does he fit into the new world order? Remember that our new world order promises include "freedom, equality and justice" "regardless of race, color, or creed:" how shall this grand ideal be translated into living reality for our own colored population?

We Yankees are quite apt to criticize the folks of Dixie for their treatment of the Negro in the South, but, as far as I can see, he does not get either economic or social justice in any section of America. He is denied membership in labor unions, and is refused employment in the main streams of American industry. He is given only such jobs as the lordly white man does not covet, and where he is tolerated in labor unions he is denied privileges of seniority, up-grading the promotion such as the Union fights to procure for its white members! His income is kept below the level of the average white worker in the same category, and he is restricted in residence to less desirable sections of our cities.

As to his social position, no more bitter cry ever came from the heart of an oppressed minority than the short but terrible sentence penned by a high school girl of Negro parentage in the City of Detroit. It is reported that the pupils were asked to write a composition setting forth their own ideas of what drastic and horrible punishment should be meted out to Hitler, if and when he is captured. This Negro lassie wrote, *"Put him in a black skin and make him live in America!"*

I know that I am decidedly out of order in talking about such things; they should be swept under the bed, concealed, and ignored. But right now I want to know *how the plan for the new world order is going to be made to work*: hence I have to ask impertinent questions. So far, I have heard no answer. I have talked to prominent sociologists, welfare workers, government experts, college professors, communists, agitators, and leaders of every variety, but have found no light on this problem. One and all the leaders of social science say, "This problem must be faced and solved." But when I ask, "How? What is *your* plan?" I am greeted with evasion or complete silence.

Thus we remind the reader of the fourth and gravest crisis that confronts the organized Church in our fateful time. Do we want to lay aside our historic mission of evangelism, and take upon our hands the solution of the problems inherent in the establishment of a new world order? If we bind ourselves to this accomplishment and the project fails, the organized church goes down with the collapse of the edifice in which she has so unwisely gambled her future! And there is great and grave danger that we will be lead into just such a tragic error. A romantic Utopianism has captivated the fancy, and controls the thinking of the prominent leaders of American Protestantism, especially those of the Liberal wing, who are apostate to

the original form of Christian Revelation. They are obsessed
with the sad delusion that America is divinely called to reform
the world, and they purpose to *force* all men to enter the
spurious heaven of the American way of life. And this regardless of whether all men want our way or not!

The convention leaders of the Northern Baptist Church,
forsaking the historic premise of the Baptist principle of the
sovereignty of the local congregation, are working desperately
to erect a political machine to influence our politicians to advance a post-war plan for a new world order. In this mis-
guided effort they are joined by the Disciples of Christ, who
also hope to affect the decisions of Congress and the peace
planners by organized propaganda and vote pressure. In this,
of course, they are only following in the steps of the Methodist
Bishops, who announced in the public press their plan to urge
all church members to write their congressmen to back the
plan *when it was presented!* Note that: the flock is expected
to give blind endorsement to a scheme, to details of which they
know nothing, thus pledging their denominational power to
certain self-appointed world statesmen, who have private
theories to advance. The Methodist Church in turn takes its
inspiration from the Federal Council of Churches, a group
which long since renounced any interest in evangelism in its
ancient form and holds no regard for the Christian principle
of regeneration. If the organized church follows this blind
leadership, it is doomed: world politics do not constitute our
mission or our field!

There is only one logical and sensible answer to the burning
question: "What place does the organized Church have in
world politics?" That answer is a terse and emphatic "none
whatever!" "Let her stay out."

To attempt political control is a dangerous game for the
church to play. History affords us the classical warning along
this line in the sad experience of the Roman Catholic Church.

In the early stages of her history, the Roman Church was aflame with missionary zeal, and her evangelists carried the Gospel to the ends of the earth. No greater annals of heroism were ever compiled than the records written by the matchless preachers of that era, who counted no sacrifice too great and no personal suffering, hardship, or loss too heavy a price, if they could win lost tribes to Christ.

But when her wealth, power, and prestige began to grow, the Popes saw a chance to gain temporal rule, and began to organize their forces into political activities instead of spiritual crusades. In the course of time Rome dominated the civilized world, and kings and emperors prostrated themselves before the papal throne and acknowledged themselves vassals of the Church. So the Roman Catholic Church became haughty, proud, self-seeking, and traded her spiritual birthright for a mess of political pottage. She gained a temporal world empire, but lost her own soul.

This deadly policy of playing world politics have persisted in the Roman strategy to the present hour, and always to her own ultimate hurt. Consider the present occupant of the Vatican, Pope Pius XII. For the sake of advancing the earthly fortunes of the papacy, he co-operated with Mussolini from the hour of the great dictator's rise to assured power. In recent months the Pope's voice has been raised in a pitiful plea for peace; but when the cohorts of Italy marched off to the rape of Ethiopia they were first blessed by the Pope, and went into the mass murder of a defenseless and unoffending people under the shield of the papal benediction. And when the conquering heroes returned, flushed with their brave and gallant conquest of tribesmen whose spears were pitifully inadequate against Italian planes, tanks and artillery, His Holiness conferred papal medals upon the conquerors!

He also gave the highest papal decoration to the bloodthirsty Antonescu, who slew 100,000 of his fellow Rumanians, most of them Jews or Protestants!

Until Hitler turned against the Roman Church, the papacy played his game for favors and added prestige, and when the German Luftwaffe was bombing prostrate London and spreading death and terror over England, no word of protest emanated from the Vatican.

But when Rome was endangered, the Pope became eloquent in his pleas for peace! He is properly horrified at the uncivilized nature of aerial warfare—but his godly feelings were never manifested until he was on the receiving end! A prisoner of the Nazis in his own sumptuous palace, he plead for justice and tolerance in dealing with the defeated: but he himself denied any such mercy to the vanquished in Spain, when Franco once again riveted the chains of papal slavery upon that unhappy land!

Does the Protestant Church want to follow this sad example? Are we ready to lay aside our spiritual warfare for the redemption of lost souls, and enter the arena of world politics, wasting our strength in the hopeless attempt to compel the world to conform to the mold of our present social theories? If we listen to the episcopate which calls itself the Federal Council of Churches we *will* make that tragic error, and will be lost in the face of the present crisis.

Is the dream of a new world order, then, in vain? Is the golden age of peace and brotherhood *never* to be realized? Not so—that great age is bound to come; and the Church of Jesus Christ will be the chief factor in bringing this happy condition to pass! The Church is really the greatest imperialistic organization on earth: we plan for a day when all the kingdoms of this earth shall be the realm of our God and His Christ, and confidently expect to see King Jesus seated upon a throne of earthly dominion, with all world rulers casting their crowns at His feet. We expect to see the new world order, but we also know that it cannot be erected without the presence and power of Christ.

Every prophet from Moses to Malachi has sung of that new world order, and the New Testament devotes a major portion of its teachings to the nature of that world rule and the manner of its consummation. Politicians and sociologists who chant this theme, are in reality plagiarists. They have evolved no new idea, but have rather perverted the ancient promise contained in God's Word, and have given their own interpretations to that promise.

The new world order is described in the eleventh chapter of Isaiah. It is not to be a democracy, a league of nations, or a Parliament of man, but is to take the form of an absolute monarchy, to which all humanity gives willing allegiance. The first verse of this descriptive prophecy identifies this coming king as an offspring of the line of King David, whose royal seed is lost in the dispersion, and so can only be identified now in Jesus Christ.

The next four verses contain an outline of the character of the King, and certainly history has never known a ruler whose benevolent and beneficent reign could qualify him under this description. Here is a promised monarch who will be governed and lead by the Spirit of God, and hence shall have complete and perfect understanding of every problem, enabling Him to render absolute and complete justice to all in His realm. Righteousness shall be the rule rather than the exception in His domain, and the instant wickedness rears its ugly head He will crush it without hesitancy or compunction. This King shall delight to argue the case of and for the meek, and the poor and humble shall be the object of His greatest interest, "regardless of creed, color, or race"!

The nature of His reign occupies the next five verses, six to nine, and every hope of every school that studies human betterment will find its fulfillment in these conditions. First, the very nature of the animal creation will be changed, and there shall be no such thing as "wild" animals on the earth, in the sense that this word is generally understood. That is to say, no animal shall hurt another or shall harm a human: and no human shall wound, hurt, or injure an animal. Pain shall be unknown in His kingdom, and the joy of life shall be guaranteed to all creatures.

Verse ten sets the bounds of this coming dominion, which shall be as universal as the extent of human habitation. Although it has a seat and center, the nations of the earth shall have equal part in this new world order, and the Jew and the Gentile alike shall serve and worship this Great Ruler.

The balance of the chapter depicts the happiness of the now-despised Jew in that coming age, and suggests certain geographical changes which help make the seat of the government accessible to all. The people of Israel are promised victory over all their ancient enemies, their traducers and their oppressors, as a pre-requisite to the inauguration of that new world order. But when this recompense has been made and adjusted, racial hatred and difference will be outlawed and forgotten. Thus Isaiah prophecies all that politicians dream of, and goes beyond their wildest hopes by promising even *more* than their theories dare contemplate.

The identity of that King is no mystery. He is described in detail in such a prophecy as Isaiah 9:6, 7. Here we read:

"For unto us a child is born, unto us a son is given: and the government shall be upon his shoulder: and his name shall be called Wonderful, Counsellor, The mighty God, The everlasting Father, The Prince of Peace. Of the increase of his government and peace there shall be no end, upon the throne of David, and upon his kingdom, to order it, and to establish it with judgment and with justice from henceforth even for ever. The zeal of the Lord of hosts will perform this."

Note those exact words and study their connotations. A "Child" is born: a "Son" is given. Luke writes of Mary's Child, who was conceived by the Holy Ghost, born, and laid in a manger. Thus the humanity of Jesus is attested. But John states: "God so love the world, He gave His only begotten Son—" and thus the deity of Jesus receives proper emphasis.

Isaiah states that this "Child-Son" is to hear the names of Deity, being entitled to such dignity as is suggested in the descriptive words: "Wonderful," "God Almighty," "Father of Eternity," "Prince of Peace." And having so identified and dignified the coming Person, the prophet then states, "And the *Government* shall be upon His shoulders."

This promise was further confirmed in Acts 1:9-11, where we read:

"And when he had spoken these things, while they beheld, he was taken up; and a cloud received him out of their sight. And while they looked stedfastly toward heaven as he went up, behold, two men stood by them in white apparel; which also said, Ye men of Galilee, why stand ye gazing up into heaven? this same Jesus, which is taken up from you into heaven, shall so come in like manner as ye have see him go into heaven."

Can any words be plainer than these? Any person who can "interpret" that passage into authority for rejecting the fact of the personal, physical, and actual return of the Saviour must have queer ideas of the meaning of the phrase "in like manner." When Jesus left this earth He had a body that was visible and ponderable to His audience, and was speaking words that were audible to their physical ears. While they gazed at and listened to Him, He ascended and was swallowed from sight by the clouds. Now, if He "so come again *in like manner*" the promise is fulfilled: if He does not, the Bible has mislead us with false promises, and is not the Word of God.

Jesus is not now called the names Isaiah said would be ascribed to Him, nor is the government committed to Him. Indeed, there is not one single government now and never has been on this earth that is wholly surrendered to Christ, and is completely dedicated to the Will of God! Nor will there be until Jesus returns to erect His throne and begins His kingdom, in which righteousness and peace will be the rule rather than the exception.

The inauguration of His reign is pre-figured and portrayed in the descriptive prophecy of Revelation 19:11-16. Note these words and carefully ponder their significance, intent, and teaching:

"And I saw heaven opened, and behold a white horse; and he that sat upon him was called Faithful and True, and in righteousness he doth judge and make war. His eyes were as a flame of fire, and on his head were many crowns; and he had a name written, that no man knew, but he himself. And he was clothed with a vesture dipped in blood: and his name is called The Word of God. And the armies which were in heaven followed him upon white horses, clothed in fine linen, white and clean. And out of his mouth goeth a sharp sword, that with it he should smite the nations: and he shall rule them with a rod of iron: and he treadeth the winepress of the fierceness and wrath of Almighty God. And he hath on his vesture and on his thigh a name written, KING OF KINGS, AND LORD OF LORDS."

Here is no "Gentle Jesus, meek and mild," and this is not a picture of a suffering Saviour, dying upon a Cross. This is a portrait of a conquering Messiah, a returning King, a victorious Monarch. For the purposes of grace and redemption of sinners, Christ did once submit to crucifixion, but for the fulfillment of prophecy and to establish His Kingdom He will yet come in power and glory. When next we see Him He is "the man on horseback"—accompanied by victorious armies, smiting His enemies and engaging in war to establish righteousness, and to cast out the usurper, Satan! Let no modern false prophet deceive you by "scholarly" interpretations which rob these words of all semblance of sense or meaning—Jesus *is* coming again, and will yet reign over this earth.

The extent and duration of that coming new world order is given in the clear statement of Revelation 20:4—"And they lived and reigned with Christ a thousand years." Those words are precise, exact, limited in meaning, and susceptible to no misunderstanding. There is to be a reign of a thousand years, and the risen dead, who were martyred for the Gospel, share that reign. This cannot refer to a heavenly throne, as that knows no end; while the definite limit of one thousand years is given to this promise. And it follows in logical sequence upon the statement of His triumphant return to earth, and all the context clearly demands an earthly locale for the fulfillment of these words.

The new world order is on its way!

Armies cannot bring it, statesmen cannot hasten it, nor can politicians delay its coming.

It will be erected as the climax of evangelism!

When the missionaries of Christ have finally carried the Gospel to every nation under heaven: when pastors and evangelists have reached their last receptive soul for the Saviour: when personal workers have won the final person who shall confess Jesus as Redeemer and Lord: then the body of Christ will be complete, and our Lord shall return from heaven to establish His Kingdom and reign over this earth.

The task of the Church is plain, being fully defined in the words of Jesus: "Go ye into all the world, and preach the Gospel to every creature." Nothing is suggested there about the Church erecting councils of nations, or dominating conferences and political assemblies. The less we, as an organization, have to do with human schemes of world betterment, the better off we will be. We have a practical, sure, God-given program for the final redemption of the race from war, poverty, oppression, and sin—let us exhaust our resources and opportunities of missionary evangelism, and thus hasten the coming of the true "new world order" wherein dwelleth righteousness and peace.

END